Analyze, act, advance

Agustín Argelich Casals

ANALYZE,
ACT,
ADVANCE

Agustín Argelich Casals

argelich

© 2015, Argelich Networks
© 2015, Agustín Argelich Casals

ARGELICH NETWORKS
Rambla Catalunya, 112
08008 Barcelona – España
Tel. (+34) 93 415 12 35
Fax. (+34) 93 217 42 98
info@argelich.com
www.argelich.com

ISBN-10: 1508580111
ISBN-13: 978-1508580119

Printed by Amazon CreateSpace

Author's photograph:
© María Eugenia Argelich Argerich

Translation:
Planet Lingua

Editorial consulting:
MarianaEguaras.com

To my dear wife, María Eugenia,
faithful and loyal companion,
always supporting me
in the good and bad,
in sorrow and joy,
always with a smile,
I find her by my side.

To my six children,
Agustín, María Eugenia, Mateo,
Nuria, Ignacio, and Benjamín,
so that they may never give up.

To my parents,
Agustín and María Pilar.

Content

Foreword   11

Part I. The challenge   **19**
1. What we are facing   21
2. A changing environment   33
3. What is efficiency   53
4. What is innovating   55

Part II. Obstacles and barriers   **63**
5. Mental laziness   65
6. The players   69
7. Envy   75
8. Procrastination   79
9. Commitment phobia   85
10. Conformity   89
11. The communication gap   93

Part III. Strategies and tools   **103**
12. What kind of tools do we have?   105
13. Attitudes and aptitudes   111
14. Hope   117
15. Proactivity and influence   123
16. Making decisions   127
17. The stool   133
18. External support   137
19. The analysis and strategy department   143
20. Selling Innovation   153

21. Negotiation   157
22. Training and self-training   167
23. Meeting management   175
24. Project development   185
25. Crisis management   203
26. Leadership in innovation processes   215
27. Information and communications
    technologies   221

Part IV. Conclusions. The life cycle   **237**
28. The servo system   239
29. Intelligent communities and organizations 245
30. The life cycle   249

Clear and distinct ideas. Quick impact list   253

A success story – Mercabarna's
telecommunication network   257

Assessment of international conferences   265

Conferences   267

Index   269

List of figures   273

References   275

Reference books   278

Recommended authors   280

Acknowledgments   281

Foreword

For twenty-five years I have been helping organizations implement the tools provided by information and communication technologies to make the most of them. I have had the opportunity to participate in many projects throughout various sectors ranging from industry to finance. I have worked on some truly meaningful and unique projects, such as the Barcelona Olympic Games in 1992, and on others that were developed in complex environments, such as a nuclear power plant. Apart from the visibility they have obtained, all projects have reached a highly important component of technological innovation, due to the fact that cutting-edge approaches have always been applied to them and that they have represented important professional challenges for those involved in them.

This already extensive professional experience, together with a reflection process on the root causes of the current social and economic situation, is included in this book of thoughts, which is both a compendium of technical training and self-taught humanism. Said humanism suggests building a culture of continuous improvement and renewal as a long-term strategy, which is not just valid in times of crisis, but also in times of growth. We must not only overcome this moment of confusion and relaunch our activity, we are also required to establish rules that minimize the possibility of similar situations recurring. We cannot continue as is.

What triggered this book was the invitation to present a paper at a conference in California in August 2010. The paper was to be about reducing costs through the use of high-capacity mobile data networks, but the organization asked me to also head a work session on the difficulties of implementing new procedures based on technological tools in companies. The truth is that the conference, which was held in San Jose, cannot be described as a resounding success, especially in terms of participation, but it was the trigger that encouraged me to capture in this book a collection of ideas and strategies that I consider useful for both people and for many organizations and companies. The very act of writing the book already means applying the culture of continuous effort it suggests, which is what led me to not feel discouraged about not meeting, in principle, the objectives I had set when accepting to participate in the conference.

At that time, I used the occasion to visit the Carmel Mission, on the Monterey Peninsula, which is located on the Pacific coast, and to pray at the tomb of the Majorcan Franciscan friar Junípero Serra Ferrer, who is considered the founder of California; in fact, his statue represents that state in the Capitol's National Statuary Hall in Washington. The spiritual bouquet I bought as a souvenir includes the imprinted motto of the nowadays beatified friar: "Always move forward and never turn back." That motto perfectly sums up this proposal for constant improvement and renewal.

In October 2011, at the conference of the Society of Communications Technology Consultants[1] held

---

[1] www.sctcconsultants.org

in Orlando, I presented a more elaborate version of the 2010 paper. The moderator, Martha Buyer[2], titled it "Moving Forward." It was widely welcomed, and several attendees encouraged me to continue working on this matter. Later, I had the opportunity to present this work in different cities, among which Amman and London.

The book is structured in four parts:

1. The challenge.
2. Obstacles and barriers to be overcome.
3. Strategies and available tools.
4. The life cycle. The attitude of constant improvement and renewal.

The first part deals with my vision of the grassroots problem that we are facing and the ecosystem it belongs to, whereas it also presents the most significant aspects and features.

The second part lists and discusses the specific difficulties we encounter every day and that hinder our progress. The barriers described are common to any project, be it of a personal or business nature, and increase the more innovative the latter is. The biggest challenge is to change one's own culture or our approach to life, be it that of an organization or of a community.

The third section presents strategies and available tools to advance and successfully carry out life, business, or innovation projects. All projects must contribute to building a better future for all. Tools are divided into three groups: philosophical, organizational, and technological ones.

_____

[2] www.marthabuyer.com

Finally, the concluding section summarizes the book's message and encourages everyone to reach their own through reflection.

I do not know how this book is going to be cataloged, I do not know if it falls into the category of management or self-help books, be it of a personal or collective nature, but I do know that, unlike other books, this has not been drafted in a business school or academia, but draws from everyday experience. It is not an academic text, but a book of reflections, which should, thus, if you will excuse the repetition, help you to reflect. It does not aim to change the life of anyone nor your organization, as many self-help manuals do. I do wish, that this book will be useful and positively influence you.

Writing a book is, definitely, to some extent, a catharsis. The author thinks that someone had to say it and, when writing it, rests assured. This is a passionately-written book, hence seeking to shake and wake you up. It is not intended to create controversy, but neither to shun the debate. It is written with energy, up to a point of outrage, and, although I have tried to avoid categorical terms, sound bites and radical approaches, some may have escaped anyway; I apologize in advance if anyone feels offended, as this is not at all the purpose.

The truth is that you never finish writing a book and that it will always be incomplete; you are not the same when you start and when you end it. Each time you re-read it you change something, as there is always an aspect that may be corrected or complemented. I accept the imperfection of the accomplished work and challenge the reader to fill in for themselves what they consider unfinished.

The book includes many concepts and ideas; some readers may feel they are too many, and, at first glance, they may even seem disconnected from each other. In fact, it is a comment I also get on my lectures: I talk too much. I agree with the criticism. Be it as it may, this is how I feel about it, and, furthermore, the goal here is not to file a doctoral treatise on a subject, but to promote reflection and continuous learning. I am, therefore, satisfied if one single idea, sentence, or concept impacts, motivates, and renews the reader.

I felt supported in this approach when reading the book by Dr. Mario Alonso Puig, *El cociente agallas* (The guts ratio), which explains how to bring out the best version of ourselves and how the creative brain works. Alonso, relying on arguments of the Scottish philosopher, David Hume, and on his deep knowledge of the workings of the human brain, stresses the ability of our brain to find a common ground between items or concepts that do not seem to have one and concludes that "invention is often an act of recombination." Hoping that the reader will find a bright idea or a motivational aspect, I have maintained this approach, so they can find more and better connections and recombinations than those I suggest. It is an innovative book, thus presenting a somewhat risky approach.

I hope I have not repeated too many concepts too often, although the basic ones are treated from different viewpoints and are recurring. We learn based on successive iterations, on mulling over the issues. The book itself means learning, starting with mine when writing it.

The reader will note that, in all chapters of this book, other works are quoted – with some exceptions, which are used as negative examples –, all of which are better than this one. They are listed in the "Reference" section. There is also a list of recommended books, which complements the former, as they are indirectly present, even if they are not mentioned in the text itself. I encourage you to consult and read them calmly, if you want to delve into a particular topic or enrich yourself in general.

I have tried to properly document the book and quote most sources, whether they are books or websites; in the latter case, I have incorporated many Internet links that worked properly at the time of publishing, but in such a volatile environment like the Internet, you never know. I apologize if any of them has stopped working. All links are listed on the book website, **www.analyze-act-advance.com**, which we will update regularly.

I put the utmost interest in writing an entertaining book, using historical facts and actual anecdotes to illustrate and introduce the various topics. I have also incorporated biblical stories and gospel accounts. I do not want to mislead anyone, this is a book of Christian inspiration.

Not only will I be happy to receive whatsoever comments, critiques (positive or negative ones), suggestions and feedback you may want to send me, but I will also appreciate them. I will try to respond appropriately and, of course, I will reply to all who write to me. For that purpose, you can use both my personal email address, agustin@argelich.com, as well as leave your opinion in the "Analyze, Act,

Advance"[3] group on LinkedIn, where you can also exchange ideas and knowledge, and connect with others that are interested in this topic.

---

[3] www.linkedin.com/groups?home=&gid=8243770

Part I

THE CHALLENGE

1. What we are facing

Houston, we have a problem.
Jack Swigert, 200,000 miles from Earth.
April 13, 1970

Recognizing the problem

To solve a problem we must first recognize that
we have one and know what it is about. Just like
astronaut Jack Swigert, who took off on Saturday,
April 11, 1970 at 13:13 hours from Cape Canaveral
(Florida, USA) en route to the moon, along with the
rest of the crew of Apollo XIII. Jack was a pilot of the
command module, but was not part of the mission, as
they had chosen him only seventy-two hours before
takeoff to replace Thomas K. Mattingly; the latter had,
apparently, been in contact with the measles virus in
the days before the launch and was not immunized, so
NASA decided not to take unnecessary risks: it must
be a real problem to get ill with measles on the Moon.
Two days later, the spaceship crew participated in a
live TV show; at the end, Jack Swigert was allowed
to stir the oxygen tanks, a common and totally un-
complicated task, but it turned out that tank no. 2
exploded and caused tank no. 1 to fail as well, and
lots of other things. They were about 200,000 miles
away from Earth. Swigert took the radio and uttered
the famous sentence, "Houston, we have a problem,"
which was a wise move. When there is a crisis or a

problem, you have to acknowledge and accept it, which is imperative to begin to solve it.

Apollo XIII returned to Earth with its three crew members safe and sound. The mission commander, James Arthur Lovell Jr., and the lunar module pilot, Fred Wallace Haise Jr., had to leave without stepping on the Fra Mauro crater, where they were supposed to land on the Moon. Jack was elected congressman from Colorado in November 1982 with 62.2% of the vote, but he did not manage to take office, because he died on December 27 due to cancer. At the Capitol, in Washington, each State is entitled to two statues of notable citizens, who are already deceased and represent the spirit and values of that State. Thus, in the visitors' lobby, just like the State of California is present in the statue of friar Junípero, that of John Leonard, Jack Swigert Jr., with his astronaut suit, represents Colorado.

It is worth reading the story regarding the causes of the problem and how it was resolved with imagination and teamwork. Eugene F., Gene, Kranz, flight director, tells this in the book *Failure is not an option*. Indeed, either they solved the problem or they would get lost in outer space. That is to say, either we fix the current situation or we are going to have a very bad time. Denying what is evident is useless; we have to accept the obstinate reality.

Accepting reality

Another historic example, in this case, to present a key factor; the lack of vision of reality. On September 1,

1939 the German army invaded Poland; thus, World War II began, which was a major disaster and a memorable crisis. The evening of that day, Colonel Kazimierz Mastalerz, commanding two squadrons of the lancers regiment no. 18 of the Pomorska Cavalry Brigade, was located on the outskirts of the city of Chojnice, in the woodland of Tuchola, about 270 km northwest from Warsaw, and ordered to attack, that is to say, he ordered a surprise charge with swords and spears against an enemy camp. The point is that he was facing the 20th motorized division of the German army, and though the Colonel relied on the advantage of the surprise factor, as well as the high mobility of his highly trained and disciplined troops, they were attacking a motorized division, that is to say, the attack was aimed against panzers and armored tanks, which were equipped with cannons and machine guns, probably the best killing machine of the time. The fact is described in the memoirs of the German General Heinz Wilhelm Guderian, Commander-in-Chief of the 19th army corps: "We were completely surrounded by the enemy north of the wooded county of Schwetz and west of Graudenz, when the Pomorska cavalry brigade, ignoring the nature of our tanks, loaded against them with swords and spears and suffered tremendous casualties."

The General's analysis is accurate: the Poles ignored or refused to accept the nature of the problem they were facing. What is more, they did not use appropriate technology; obviously, you do not defeat a tank with a spear. Though, undoubtedly, the lancers regiment no. 18 of the Pomorska cavalry brigade had guts, they could not so much as tickle the Germans.

Colonel Mastalerz was killed in that line of duty. He and his men became myths, like the heroes they were, but they failed and were defeated. I think they had better options and their case is an example of the fact that denying that we have a problem, not accepting reality and not using the right technology hinder, if not prevent, the resolution of many issues.

The crisis we are experiencing

The current problem is not restricted to an economic crisis. The crisis is the fever, the manifestation of the disease, and is not just the result of financial speculation, but has deeper causes arising from the fading values that underpin society. Behind speculation or the search for quick and unscrupulous wealth there is a vice that is called greed or, putting it another way, there is lack of a virtue called temperance, but, above all, there is a lack of wisdom and common sense, which is due to the fact that the reality of life is not accepted and, instead, people tend to believe that it is possible to get rich quickly and effortlessly. This is an excessively short-termed vision that lacks valuation of a work well done, as a popular saying goes: "Easy (money) in, easy (money) out."

Basically, we face a culture that is deeply rooted in a significant part of society and is characterized by the absence of meaning in life and lack of motivation: we just get by. Said culture is transverse, in other words, it is uniformly distributed, hence infiltrating companies and all human organizations, including religious ones, and translates into thinking we deserve everything we wish, that we have a right to it effortlessly.

An example of that model is the replacement of an information channel with a high degree of professionalism, such as CNN+, with the 24-hour Big Brother channel. That is, information reports or discussions are replaced by the public exposure of a group of people locked in a house, who are being lazy, with the resulting coexistence problems, giving free rein to their instincts and emotions, without any control. We are shown people that are living in a stabled manner, and at the time they even dared to defend an alleged sociological interest of this approach. It is simply about observing a group of people with *no* studies, *no* job *nor* willing to do any of these. "It is my parents' problem, who brought me into the world without consulting me," a member of this group told a person who asked him about his attitude towards life. I should clarify that I first used the term "generation", but it is clearly unfair and disproportionate, since there are many young people who do not share that approach at all. By the way, *no-no-nor* people are sometimes also called *nor-high*[4], that is to say, they have not even completed compulsory secondary education.

Some people are interested in keeping us entertained, in case we start to think and reflect. We should not allow

Some people are interested in keeping us entertained

---

[4]   In Spanish "ni-eso", and ESO is "obligatory secondary school". In fact, these people have not finished the high (secondary) school.

the construction of an entertainment society. One thing is to have fun and rest and another to be idle and unfocused, avoiding to accept life as it is and to consider new challenges. Therefore, we must take good care not to get distracted with the circus, as the Romans did with their shrewd emperors, when things were not doing well, "bread and circuses for the people": a few Christians, who thought differently, thrown to the lions, and everyone was entertained.

A manifestation of that culture are also Malthusian theories ("we will starve to death"). In that sense, a modern or neo-Malthusian expression are doomsday exaggerations about climate change. They say it is irreversible and that we will freeze or fry to death, or that weather phenomena of apocalyptic proportions will appear. The error of Thomas Malthus is to deny the capacity for progress and improvement that the new tools offer to face our problems. Malthus, who incidentally was an Anglican reverend, was very influential in his time and still is, because pessimism and misfortune sell well. It is very easy to say that there is no solution. It is a great excuse for our convenience, to justify laziness. It is the dark side. One thing is to accept and acknowledge that there are problems and difficulties, but quite another is to assume that there is no solution. Basically, this attitude denies change and improvement and, from a theological point of view, even denies redemption, which is

> One thing is accept difficulties and another completely different is consider there is no solution

quite surprising for a cleric. But that is not the subject of this book. A sample of the irrationality of Malthus' theories is that he even wrote that "a man who is born into a world already possessed has no claim of right to the smallest portion of food, and, in fact, has no business to be where he is. At nature's mighty feast there is no vacant cover for him. She tells him to be gone and will quickly execute her own orders." It has been almost two hundred years since Malthus died, and, for the time being, we are still here and are many more, but he somehow anticipated the culture of waste which Pope Francis warns us about[5].

In the West, a clear manifestation of that neo-Malthusian culture are major demographic changes that lead to aging caused by two diverging trends; falling birth rates and rising life expectancy. These changes will have a brutal impact on the economy and will force major changes to the wrongly called "welfare state." The fall in the birth rate, which is already well below the replacement rate (2.1 children per woman of childbearing age); in 2012, the birth rate was 1.32 in Spain and 1.58 in Europe; both figures are a clear sign of the prevailing pessimism and lack of confidence in the future, in oneself and in others. Moreover, the fall of the birth rate is closely linked to the delay in the age at which people marry and the instability of that relationship. The fear of commitment, decision-making, and the future manifests itself unequivocally. Maybe we are indeed poorly adapted to the environment and, as Darwin

---

[5]   Interview with Henrique Cymerman in *La Vanguardia*, 06/13/2014.

said, only the best-adapted species will survive. Luckily, we are able to rectify. To learn more about the demographic situation it is essential to read the reports that are regularly published by the Spanish Institute for Family Policy[6], headed by Eduardo Hertfelder. This institute enjoys special consulting status with the United Nations Economic and Social Council (ECOSOC)[7].

Another example of the current trend is the book *Hello Laziness* by Corinne Maier. As the subtitle of the work reads, it is about the art and the need to do as little as possible in the company; in fact, it explains, from its author's personal experience at Électricité de France, how to go unnoticed in a large company for fifteen years. The book was very controversial at the time, particularly in France, but we all know that it reveals an undeniable fact, that this is the civil service mentality taken to its extreme against the concept of public servant. The pandemic spread of that mentality is much to blame for the current situation. Actually, it is not surprising at all that the second book of the author was *No Kids. 40 Good Reasons Not to Have Children*. By the way, both books are not worth reading, because, at bottom, they do not say anything new; about laziness and selfishness, we all know pretty much.

There are several studies on Spanish society, such as "Alerta y desconfianza. La sociedad española ante la crisis" (Alert and distrust. The Spanish society in the crisis), published by Víctor Pérez-Díaz and Juan Carlos

---

[6]   www.ipfe.org

[7]   www.un.org/es/ecosoc

Rodríguez, who confirm that apathetic mindset. Some data quoted from this work may suffice:

- 69% of the population believes that, in Spain, most people only do their job as required.
- 76.7% of Spaniards believe that here the success of others arouses suspicion and that they tend not to recognize it.
- 56.6% of people believe that the most important thing to be rich is to have contacts and cultivate them. Only 17.8% of respondents appreciated having good ideas and striving to implement them.

My opinion is that the people who have been asked were not sincere enough. Compliance means to "comply" and "lie." I make see that I am busy and they make see that they pay me, a doctor at a large hospital told me. It is quite scary. Passing grades are given away under the guise of equal opportunity and those who excel are punished. Just wait and see when we go from envy to emulation, as professor Javier Fernández Aguado says. It seems not so difficult to understand that the more wealth is generated around us, the more there will be to share. Nobody has the same talents nor the same number of talents; the important thing is to multiply them for the good of all, not bury them[8].

> Let's move from envy to emulation
>
> *Javier Fernández Aguado*

---

[8]   The Parable of the Talents, Matthew 25, 14-30. Although the talents of the parable are a coin, Christian tradition has never interpreted the parable literally (economically), but the talents must be understood as

Basically, we face a lack of meaning and values, which in the business field manifests itself in passive attitudes; it is the attitude of "I am a nobody," "they ignore me," "I am alienated," which leads you to not identify with the goals of the company. Sometimes, these attitudes are directly or indirectly promoted by the management and may be tackled by a culture of constant improvement and renewal, as well as by pursuing a policy of constant innovation that seeks the efficiency of business processes and generates wealth. Passivity affects all organizational levels and generates a lack of projects and investments, as personal attitudes are propagated to the attitude of groups, businesses, and even societies.

Viktor Frankl, a Jewish Viennese psychiatrist, founder of logotherapy[9] and survivor of several Nazi death camps, establishes the concept of collective neurosis in his famous book *Man's Search for Meaning*. What is more, he considers that the existential vacuum is the collective neurosis of our time and describes that existential vacuum as "a private and personal form of nihilism, for nihilism can be defined as the contention that being has no meaning." Frankl is categorical, I would even say harsh,

> The existential vacuum is the collective neurosis of our time
>
> *Viktor Frankl*

---

the natural capabilities, skills or abilities that each one of us has or, from a Christian perspective, that we receive from God.

[9] Logotherapy is known as the third Viennese school, the other two are those founded by Freud and Jung.

with his analysis, but also extremely realistic.

Adding value, contributing something is the goal here. Not resigning. "If you do not move forward, you move back," said Saint Augustine. We cannot settle for maintaining the achievements, with zero growth approaches, for the simple reason that history confirms that they are decreasing approaches. If you do not add, you subtract. Attack is the best form of defense. Immobility leads to collapse. A recent example is communist systems. Keeping the rules of the game, when circumstances have changed, makes no sense.

> If you do not move forward, you move back
>
> *Saint Augustine*

Barack Obama won an election with the famous slogan "Yes, we can" to overcome pessimism and renew hope. Assuming that we can, we must obviously take a step forward, make the decision, say yes, we do and carry it out. As John Fitzgerald Kennedy said in his famous speech, in which he announced the space race: "We choose to go to the Moon, not because it is easy, but because it is hard,"[10] we decide to tackle a challenge.

A combination of great labor and social rights and low productivity, caused by low motivation, is unaffordable. You cannot keep red tape tasks and, to make matters worse, execute them analogously, since they only hinder entrepreneurship and business

---

[10] Original speech in English on er.jsc.nasa.gov/seh/ricetalk.htm. The video of the speech can be seen on youtu.be/ouRbkBAOGEw.

development. Bureaucratic and inflexible administrative superstructures, such as municipalities, counties, provinces, autonomous regions, the State and the European Union, are technologically outdated. We must, therefore, rectify the situation, strike a balance between rights and obligations, as well as freedom and responsibility.

Having analyzed the situation, you look for alternatives, which indeed exist, and apply them. That is what this book seeks to promote.

2. A changing environment

Those individuals survive
that are best adapted
to their environment.
Charles Darwin

I believe that, to properly understand the problems we are facing, we should delve into the changes that have occurred in recent years on the planet and, in particular, in the Western world and in Spain in a marked way.

In fact, this chapter describes the environment in which we operate, which, to my knowledge, a significant part of society has not seen nor understood, as many companies have not. Charles Darwin stated that only those individuals survive that are best adapted to their environment, so let us see what the latter looks like.

An inverted pyramid

The birth pyramid in European countries is already shaped like an inverted pyramid. That is, new generations have fewer and fewer members, whereas the top of the pyramid (the elderly) grows in height and width (Figure 1). This trend began decades ago. Thus, we are living longer and we want to continue living with high levels of quality and autonomy; but taking care of our elderly requires both financial and human resources.

Figure 1. Population pyramid of Spain as of January 1, 2013.

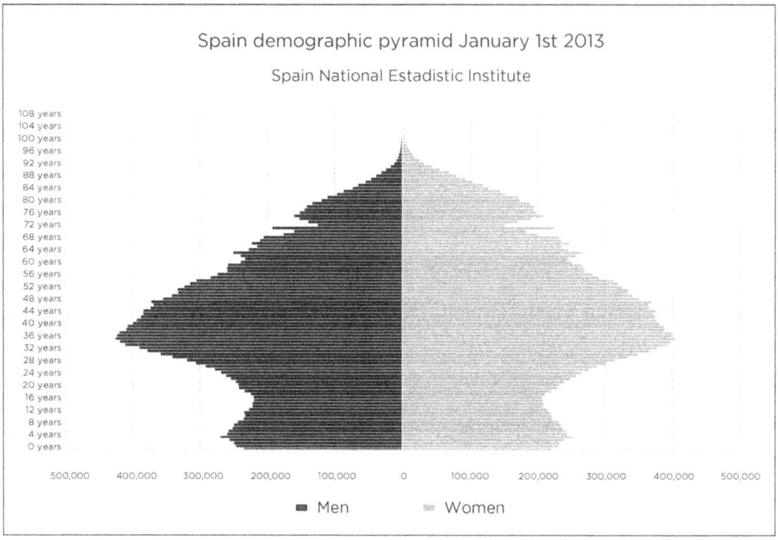

Spain demographic pyramid January 1st 2013

Spain National Estadistic Institute

Note that the age group with most individuals (36 years) includes 828,438 people and the one with less (17 years) only 425,122 people. That is to say, in round figures, there are half of people aged 17 compared to people aged 36. Demographic data for Spain are available from the Spanish National Statistics Institute (www.ine.es).

The survival of our society requires that the birth rate is restored. To recover the replacement rate it is not only necessary to have an economic upturn, but also a transcendent view valuing motherhood and the continuity of our society via our children.

The inverted pyramid and greater wealth in Western societies, enhanced by the impact of speculative economic bubbles, have caused a pull effect. We needed more people to support our growth, and here there were no newborns, and still are none.

Immigration may help, but, on its own, cannot put up with the challenge and is not a cheap solution, as it entails important integration challenges.

Digital natives

Technological change from the analog to the digital era, from the atom economy to a mixed economy, with the emergence of the bit economy, is a process that recent generations have not gone through. For our children this is nothing new, they were born into it ready-made; therefore, it is not true that they have already accepted this change, as they have not even seen it.

Enrique Dans, professor at IE Business School in Madrid, in his book *Todo va a cambiar. Tecnología y evolución: adaptarse o desaparecer* (Everything will change. Technology and evolution: adapt or disappear), encourages everyone to ask themselves what part of a business are bits and how many are atoms. My opinion is that the title's statement is too categorical and that not everything is going to change; although many things are indeed changing and will change, forgotten aspects will also revive, such as timeless values and age-old wisdom.

For the first time in history, many innovations are taken on first by new generations and people than by companies. Social networks are a strong example of that. Let us comment on a very specific aspect, the concept of presence. My teenage children declare their current state on messaging systems in a natural way (I am busy, available, etc.). Sometimes, they even declare their state innocently. For example, in the messaging application on my smartphone I have incorporated some of my children,

> Digital natives are the new clients and the new workforce

and, recently, as one of them went out partying, his state was "Busy, I am partying." I requested him to send me immediately a more detailed description of his state. Conversely, within a company you must explain to the whole organization what your presence means, what use there is if you say that you are or are not available and, additionally, you must detail for what type of communication or through which channel.

We must educate the organization, sell the benefits of the new tools, promote proper training and provide the necessary adjustment period. These aspects should be taken into account now, because digital natives are the new customers and the new partners. Companies should consider how younger generations communicate and work, because they do so differently from those who have preceded them.

Digital natives include a large number of only children. Childhood experiences are not the same for an only child and for one growing in a large family; the dedication of parents and grandparents is not the same either. Furthermore, the experiences of living with siblings, or lack thereof, are important factors that influence the character of a child. Their experience in a period of growth and prosperity without major crises will also influence how they tackle difficulties. So, what motivates our children? It is obvious that difficulties harden and build more resilient people.

Reconciling personal and professional life

We must address how we balance the time spent working and that dedicated to personal and family life. At the household level, we are facing a double challenge; on the one hand, caring for our elders and, on the other, for our children.

Is it wise to waste two hours a day commuting to work to sit in front of a computer and a phone? How many more positive things than being stuck in a traffic jam, burning fuel and polluting the environment, may be done for two hours?

I can think of some, starting with spending more time with your children while helping them, for example, to do their homework. In addition, practicing sports, reading, meditating, praying, or talking with friends, among other things.

Considering working at home or nearby in friendly environments that are already being established (co-working in shared working centers[11]) is not only a smart solution, but almost mandatory. How much stress would we avoid?

Production methods and workplace relations. Aligned or alienated

The industrial revolution of the 19th century with the mass migration of rural population to the cities to join as production line workers, under harsh working conditions, and the resulting social tensions led to a labor law and a certain culture of relations between the company and the employee. Class unions and Marxist utopia emerged, which ended up falling apart,

---

[11] www.coworkingspain.es

literally, with the fall of the Berlin Wall on Thursday night, November 9, 1989.

Despite the vicissitudes of history, a culture of confrontation between employer and employee still persists, as well as a labor law which is based on the paradigms of the industrial revolution of the 19th century. The said legislation protects the rights of workers from abuses that occurred at that time and is designed for a system of very long-term relationships. The employee carried out a routine job for years. The company virtually controlled the lives of their employees; remember, for example, that in the textile colonies enterprises facilitated housing and schooling, and even saw to it that religious care was ensured. The objectives of the worker and the employer were not sufficiently aligned. Marx speaks of alienation, submission, exploitation.

But, in the 21st century, such a relationship does not make sense. How do we feel about our company or organization: alienated or aligned? If Marx is right and we feel alienated, that is, exploited, then we are not doing so well. If, however, employees are in line with the objectives of the company, the latter will fare better and the staff will feel more rewarded as well. That is to say, you have to row together to make the canoe advance, especially when navigating through troubled waters, such as a crisis. A colleague of mine told me: "I have a partner that is scoring in our own goal," that is, instead of adding to it, he is subtracting. The choice is clear: either he changes or he cannot continue, because it is essential that everyone contributes. No one can subtract.

In life you have to be aligned with regard to several aspects, yourself, your family, your company, your country. We will leave the first two for another time. Let us focus on business, which is where I think there is a very serious problem. The argument also serves for the concept of nation, if it is understood as the joint venture of all citizens. As long as large segments of society consider that the objectives of a company and those of the workers are not the same, we are going wrong. As long as the employer is deemed an exploiter rather than an individual, who, with greater or lesser leadership capacity and risking his money, is able to generate wealth for the benefit of all and not just for his own, we are not doing well. You cannot perform, if you consider that you are there, because you have no other choice. Riaz Khadem, author, among other books, of *Total Alignment,* teaches us that the objectives of shareholders, managers, employees, customers, and suppliers must be aligned, that is to say, a win-win situation which everyone profits from. In a discussion, I accused him of being utopian and of posing an impossible goal, and he said that reality would impose that model. That is, either we all make businesses work, hence our society, or we will encounter a system that does not work and is doomed to self-destruction. Systems do not take it all, a continuous accumulation of inefficiencies leads to collapse. Evil destroys itself, said John Paul II, the problem is that sometimes degeneration occurs gradually and goes unnoticed. Let us recall that either you advance or you recede, as Saint Augustine taught us, we cannot stay still. The more synchronized the rowing team is, the faster the boat moves. A common goal is essential. In this environment, there is no need to comment on a union call for a demonstration against employers: this is about wanting to apply 19th-century approaches to 21st-century problems, they are not aligned. It is an outdated approach.

Speed of change

Changes occur increasingly faster, as they accelerate. The life of many products and services shortens. A clear example: mobile telephony has grown from being non-existent to saturating the market in just a few years, with cases like Spain, where market penetration exceeds 100%, there is more than one line per person. Even within that industry, market-leading companies have disappeared and been replaced by others in a few years. The first mobile phones were called "Motorola", then Nokia reigned for some years, which gave way to BlackBerry and this succumbed to Apple and Samsung smartphones and those of other Asian manufacturers.

Another prime example is the disappearance of the film roll. It is not that we do not take pictures, much to the contrary, the number of pictures taken has grown exponentially, but they are no longer developed; at most, some of them are printed from time to time. And the funniest thing is that it was a Kodak engineer on a payroll, Steven Sasson, with the support from his supervisor, Gareth A. Lloyd, who invented digital photography in 1975, but Kodak itself failed to adapt. The problem was not that they did not innovate, but that they were unable to adapt their business model to the innovations that they were generating themselves. Instead of adapting, they let others take the lead and compete against them with their own inventions, while they were still thinking that the roll and photographic paper would remain forever after. On January 17, 2012, the Eastman Kodak Company filed for protection under Chapter 11, which is the equivalent of bankruptcy; now it undergoes restructuring to reinvent itself. Late and badly, they could have started in 1975.

What is indisputable is that change will not stop nor slow down in all areas.

The need for continuous change

The difference between Steve Jobs and the managers at BlackBerry is that the latter had a great idea, email on the move, whereas Steve Jobs had a collection of great ideas consecutively. It no longer suffices to have a great idea, enjoy it, and rest on one's laurels, as it can be extremely short-lived. It is very interesting to read the article published in the Canadian newspaper *The Globe and Mail*[12] on the ins and outs of BlackBerry's fall. Slow decision-making, disagreements in the management team, not listening to their major customers, such as Verizon, and lack of leadership, among other errors.

Energy and geopolitical changes

Nothing works without energy. It is at the base of the pyramid. We can get everything with energy. If

---

[12] http://www.theglobeandmail.com/report-on-business/the-inside-story-of-why-blackberry-is-failing/article14563602/?page=all

the cost of energy increases, so does the cost of all products.

Europe's energy dependence is a brake and a big risk. The ideological overload in the current energy model should be reconsidered, such as, for example, the nuclear power moratorium or the ban on fracking[13] in some regions of Europe. Any strategy aimed at optimizing the use of energy is not only accurate, but should also be enhanced.

A wrong energy policy causes a huge wealth to be transferred to countries with other values. This is money that in those countries is often not used for the benefit of its own people and that in the West could be used in other fields. Europe is bleeding economically, because it refrains from having its own energy. However, the development of fracking in the United States has provided the country with energy independence, so that it no longer needs oil from the Middle East, which is a geostrategic shift of major proportions.

The energy supply model should also be modified by the deployment of smart grinds[14], a large number of micro power centers (even at a home level) that were connected to the public power distribution network and managed in an intelligent and coordinated way, because all of them are connected to a telecommunications network.

---

[13] Fracking: techniques for obtaining hydrocarbons by hydraulic fracture of rocks containing them.

[14] The consolidation of these solutions in Spain is being affected by protectionist regulations in favor of large generating companies.

Major innovations and changes in the world of energy are arising.

Transportation

Advances in communications have been spectacular in recent years. In less than a day, we can reach almost any point on the globe, where until recently it took months to arrive at. People who would make their fortune in the Americas rarely came back.

The distances between cities are shortened with the construction of high-speed trains.

Moreover, low-cost flights make it very easy and extremely economical to fly from one place to another, especially with regard to those that are at a middle distance.

The excessive increase in the cost of energy will make them more expensive again, which may cause us to rethink our offshoring policies.

On another level, work at home or close to home also requires less transportation.

Sociopolitical changes

The collapse of communist systems, the failure of a highly planned economy, launches hundreds of millions of people, who legitimately aspire to escape poverty, to which inefficient and dictatorial regimes had condemned them, into a productive economy. Thus, the number of potential consumers, as well as competitors, increases.

The demographic weight of Asia, with India and China each exceeding one billion inhabitants, provides a high production capacity and, in turn, opens markets with a huge growth potential. Power is shifting eastward, after a predominance of the Christian West during merely five hundred years, which started with the discovery of America.

The awakening of the Arab world, much of which was under socialist dictatorships, is an awakening of enlightened and professional sectors, and, although it is in danger of being capitalized by Islamic fundamentalist sectors, the latter are certainly not those who have led or provoked it. The influence of communication technologies on the whole process is undeniable. I use the word «awakening», because I believe it best describes the attitude of a society which was numbed under the weight of its dictatorships.

Telecommunications networks and globalization

The ability to communicate via electronic means is very high and inexpensive. Over the Internet, it is possible to maintain and establish contact with many people, no matter where they are physically located, even recover old relationships and establish new ones, based on common interests or hobbies.

Until very recently, it was not possible to access vast amounts of data instantly, with virtually no cost, anywhere. Any Internet user can publish and make their contents, ideas, and works accessible. The control over the media is lost, the unidirectional message from a few to many becomes one from all to all. Television and newspapers lose their power with regard to Twitter, Facebook, and blogs.

Internet is the great discussion forum. It is the agora of the world, the global senate, the main square of the global village. Improving communication between cultures and communities, which will lead to a better mutual understanding and greater ease of dealing with others; consequently, conflicts will decrease, whereas trade and collaboration opportunities will increase. And, as we all know, regular contact brings affection: thanks to the Internet there will be fewer wars. The clash and confrontation of ideas on the Internet will be very positive.

A successful message or a good song can succeed with virtually no promotional costs. We could call it the "Leopoldo effect," by which I mean Leopoldo Abadía[15], who is an example of how a brilliant writing of a retired professor, virally transmitted over the Web, launches its author to an unprecedented success, who ends up writing three books and being a speaker who is overwhelmed by demand.

The ability to copy a document, a photo, or a video and immediately launch it for everyone to see is awesome. The protection of intellectual property, currently based on a pay-per-copy system, gets complicated. The copying industry is about to become extinct.

Moreover, the concepts of privacy and modesty will change. Locating personal or private data is very easy and, in most cases, it is owing to the fact that the

---

[15] www.leopoldoabadia.com

people concerned have exposed them recklessly. You have to be careful with what you write on Facebook. There is a danger of trivializing privacy and that the number of contacts causes a loss in friendship quality. A Facebook friend is certainly not a friend; he or she is an acquaintance, somebody that, at some point, has crossed your path with more or less influence and with whom an indeterminate and quite hazy link was established.

Watching TV has gone from being an activity that happened in the family or in a group, and with a wide yet local range, to constituting a personal, à-la-carte, and global matter. Television is broadcasted over the Internet. All channels on Earth are within our reach, and we visualize them on an array of devices, smartphones, tablets, personal computers, or conventional TV sets; you can watch TV on any device connected to a telecommunications network. The Internet has defeated conventional television. Digital terrestrial television (DTT) is late. Television is becoming a matter of personal consumption.

The digital economy: a bits and people's economy

Digital economy will focus more on the customer than on the product. Customer service will be paramount.

We have gone from an economy based on producing many user-friendly goods to another which focuses on generating goods that include many possibilities, can be configured and customized, that is to say, can be adapted to the peculiarities and needs of each client (in short, customization). A clear example of this are computer applications that must be parameterized, hence training and customer/user service are critical. In their book *The One to One Future,* American consultants Don Peppers and Martha Rogers talk about the revolution in customer relationships, stating that interaction is increasingly intense and critical. The important thing is to establish a personal, one-to-one relationship with the client and build long-term relationships. These authors delve into this line in the book *Rules to Break & Laws to Follow,* where they advocate to overcome the shortsightedness with which many companies are run.

The customer is gaining more and more power. Enrique Dans speaks of a neo-Humanism that evolves thanks to the technological revolution.

Working on net, in multidisciplinary teams and per project

The digital economy, the knowledge economy, the value-added economy, the customer-focused economy, internationalization and globalization, along with changes and social challenges, such as reconciling family and professional life, are already generating a different way of working and tackling new projects.

These new projects are increasingly complex, and their development must take into account many factors. Reality cannot be seen from a single viewpoint. For

---
Reality is
polyhedral
---

example, if we observe a simple object like a glass from the top, we see a circle, but if we look at it laterally, a rectangle appears; neither of the two images represent the glass reality. In real life, geometry is far richer, reality is polyhedral (multifaceted), it has many sides. To understand it as well as possible, we should look at it from different angles and different points of view.

When approaching an improvement or renovation project, we must have several specialists at hand. You have to rely on the participation of various departments within the organization (commercial, technical, legal, human resources, etc.), which should ensure we have an overview of the issues that need to be addressed. Projects are also becoming more international, as businesses become global, as you have to sell in as many countries as possible. Projects are already involving people living in several countries, in other time zones, not sharing their mother tongue and belonging to different cultures.

In this new framework, organizations cannot afford large and rigid structures, giant and inefficient systems. Starting with the Administration, they should move towards more agile and flexible models. Teams will be set up to work on specific projects, which are targeted and limited in time and will be attended by expressly hired professionals from different countries, including more than one continent. Networking will occur using Unified Communications and Collaboration (UC2) tools[16] in multicul-

---

[16] www.ucstrategies.com

tural and mul-tidisciplinary teams, which will be set up for a specific purpose and will disintegrate as soon as this is achieved.

A real example of this will be enlightening: in May 2011 I established, thanks to the Barcelona Mobile World Congress, a partnership between my company and a Canadian company. Taking advantage of the invitation to participate in the Conference of the Canadian Telecommunications Consultants Association[17] in Ottawa, it occurred to me to stop by in Montreal in order to meet the company's president and staff. The sales manager offered to pick me up at the hotel early in the morning. As we were driving to a town in the outskirts and passing by a business park, he pointed out that there had been their headquarters, but that they closed it. I asked him if they had outgrown it and had to move to a bigger place, and he explained that it was not at all like that, that it had been closed, because everyone worked at home and they did not need it. It did not make sense to pay a rent for a weekly meeting. The management team met on Fridays for dinner at a nice restaurant. To sum up, instead of going to the headquarters we ended up in the president's home. Out of discretion, I will not describe the house nor say how many cars and which models were parked there; I will only say that, apparently, it worked.

The president, an engineer of Iranian origin, told me that he decided that everybody would gain, if they started to work at home. That it made no sense wasting two hours a day stuck in traffic to get to the

---

[17] www.ctca.ca

office. The whole team is permanently connected using unified communication tools, and, apart from the engineers working in the Montreal area, many work in different US cities. In addition, there are entire software development teams in Russia, India, and South Africa. This is a company with a proven track record that has found highly advanced solutions, through which the management of millions of mobile phone lines has been optimized. It has also significantly reduced travel to visit clients, large telecommunications carriers, with whom they meet by video conference. Anecdotally, I was told that the Friday meetings to have dinner are never canceled, which in winter and in Montreal means quite a lot. They are not canceled even with a polar storm raging and a temperature of minus 20 degrees Celsius. It is really interesting to work with companies with that mentality and it is obvious that they are the future. By the way, I was told that they were lacking engineers.

An exciting time

We could write a lot about the changes we are facing, we have only mentioned a few, but the summary is that we are going to enjoy a time of multicultural encounters, information flow, quick, agile, flexible, full of opportunities and risks, of things that have worked for a long time and are no longer useful, of excesses and rebalancing. Do we have the right attitude to deal with them? I think we do not or, at least, not every-one. Conformist culture, with commitment phobia, excessive entertainment culture (keep entertained, lest you start thinking), and individualism, based on reactivity and non-cooperation, is the manifestation of a true crisis, with a background, and which can be addressed with a culture of continuous improvement. I think we have strategies and appropriate mental and technological tools to deal with it and overcome the current situation.

Don Tapscott, an expert in business strategy over the Internet and author of the popular books on digital economy *Wikinomics* (bestselling in the US) and *Grown Up Digital (The Digital Age)*, says: "This is not a crisis, it is a historic change,"[18] and the relationship of five aspects which, in his opinion, will shape the new model is quite interesting:

- Collaboration
- Openness and transparency
- Interdependence
- Sharing intellectual property
- Integrity

We are not facing a difficult time, since all times are in their own way, but an exciting one, in which our great opportunity has not yet arrived. In fact, I think that stating that we are living in the worst time or in one of the worst times in the history of mankind

> We now have the best technology, as well as the best communication and the best knowledge between human beings, we have ever had

---

[18] Interview in *La Vanguardia*, 21/12011.

is complete nonsense. All times have been very difficult, and, certainly, many of those who have experienced them have considered them horrible times. You just need a little historical perspective to realize that we now have the best technology, as well as the best communication and the best knowledge between human beings, we have ever had. For example, we do not seem to be on the brink of nuclear destruction, as this has been the case at some point. Here, nobody even remembers the Cold War anymore, nor a 20th century plagued by wars and tragedies. We face great challenges and we have more resources than ever to address them. Do we actually want to address them?

3.   What is efficiency

Being efficient is working smartly.

Acting efficiently is acting smartly. Being efficient is doing something well with no waste of time nor energy. This means devoting to each case the time and resources it requires, no more no less.

Being efficient does not mean being a perfectionist. Perfection is rarely attained. In some matters, such as studies and projects, it is clear that there are always things that can be improved, expanded, rethought, but at some point you have to consider them closed. Efficient people know when to choose that time. A proverb explains this very well: "Perfection is the enemy of good." In fact, perfectionism is very dangerous, it is a neurosis.

Do not confuse efficiency with effectiveness. Being effective is doing something well and getting the expected results. That is to say, to be efficient you have to be more than just effective. Efficiency is, therefore, essential to be highly productive.

For a process to be not only effective, but also efficient, it needs to be designed appropriately. A process that was efficient when it was established does not necessarily

> Being efficient is doing something well with no waste of time nor energy

remain so over time, because circumstances and the available tools change. We can take a picture with an SLR camera with a film roll or with a digital camera. Both devices are effective, as both are used to get a picture. But, in the first case, it is necessary to develop the roll and pass the photo onto paper and, in the second case, it is not. Digital cameras are much more efficient, we take many more pictures, it is very easy and inexpensive to obtain copies and distribute them.

Thus, to maintain efficiency, you have to go into a periodic reassessment of the processes we have in place. This job reassessment is called process re-engineering. In the software world, this is intrinsic, as new versions are constantly being developed.

Stephen Covey wrote a well-known book, *The 7 Habits of Highly Effective People.* That is to say, he was referring to people who do things right; the adverb "highly" can be understood in the sense that they do a lot of things and even do them very well. Somehow, we could say that a highly effective person is an efficient person. Obviously, I recommend reading this and other works by Covey. We are going to mention the seven habits throughout this book.

I insist that working efficiently means working smartly, and for that analysis is essential. Analyze the problem before starting to work on it. When discussing the steps a project should have, we shall insist that the analysis stage is vital for its success.

4. What is innovating

Christopher Columbus
was an innovator,
not a discoverer.

Innovating is doing something differently than usual or established. Innovation must pursue that the process is carried out more efficiently, using fewer resources, without wasting any time or energy.

Christopher Columbus was an innovator who discovered America by accident. He was not looking for a new continent, but for a shorter way to get to the Indies; therefore, he questioned how something was done and looked for a more efficient solution. He was an open-minded person and was highly successful, not the way he expected, but much more. His innovative zeal really contributed a lot to humankind.

Many of the business processes were established long ago, in different circumstances than the current ones and with a different availability of resources and tools. Innovation is, therefore, not about questioning previous decisions, which adds nothing; obviously, you cannot rewind time, the past cannot be changed. In fact, it is a waste of time to regret an earlier decision which has resulted in an inefficient process; what you have to do is to work so that it may be efficient again as soon as possible and generate wealth, not loss. When a process has been established for some time, you always have to question it.

Research & Development & Innovation

There is a wide range of improvements to daily processes

Sometimes, we think that research, development, and innovation (R&D&I) only refer to the pursuit of scientific advances or the development of new technologies and we forget that there is a wide range of improvements to daily processes.

Another common confusion is to mix up research and development and innovation. When speaking of R&D&I, we stop too often at the first word, research, and downplay development and innovation. Research provides us with new knowledge and tools; with development and innovation said knowledge and tools are used to solve real solutions and get practical applications. All aspects are needed. The best and most clarifying definition I know is that by Julio Lorca Gómez and Alejandro Jabad, quoted in the Spanish Wikipedia article[19] defining R&D&I:

Innovation is investing knowledge to obtain value

"Research is investing resources to gain knowledge, while innovation is investing knowledge to obtain value." It seems that this definition was inspired by one of the former Finnish Prime Minister Esko Aho,

---

[19] es.wikipedia.org/wiki/Investigacion_desarrollo_e_innovacion

which is really provocative and exceedingly materialistic and states as follows: "Research is investing money to gain knowledge, while innovation is investing knowledge to obtain money."

> We are all called to innovate

From that magnificent definition follows that, while research is not available to everyone, innovation is indeed, as we all have knowledge in some field and can, therefore, generate value with it. Based on our knowledge and capabilities, not only can we all innovate, but we are all called to innovate.

Moreover, we cannot forget that an appropriate strategy for R&D&I creates a virtuous circle; it is a feedback phenomenon, a servosystem. This is one of the key ideas on which this entire book evolves.

Innovation means to always evolve

The innovative process should be an evolution, not a revolution in itself; it can produce revolutionary results, but does not have to destroy, in principle, nothing that is working, that is effective, but not efficient. It should allow a smooth transition, without any break-up, from the previous to the new situation. Things cannot stop working, because it is always better to run inefficiently than not working at all. You cannot stop day-to-day business.

> Innovation must be an evolution, not a revolution

Risk can be managed

Moreover, risk is inherent to any innovation process. That means that things can go wrong, but that something can go wrong does not mean that it should not be done. Risk can be managed. You can take actions to minimize it, but it should not be denied. We must accept that zero risk does not exist.

Details are important

Often drastic improvements are achieved by changing small details. We must assert the importance of little things and of work that remains unseen.

There are many things, which are not seen, but are there. You cannot see, for example, the love of a husband for his wife or children, but it exists and countless things happen because of it. The philosophical school of phenomenology[20] studies these aspects, the visible and invisible component of each phenomenon. The culture of a company is not seen either, but it exists, and the same goes for motivation.

We often do not see the people who clean the office, but no one would work at ease if it were dirty.

---

[20] School of philosophy founded by the Jew Edmund Husserl. It is one of the most influential philosophical movements of the 20th century and even of the 21st. Transcendental phenomenology studies phenomena and says that they include what is seen and what is not seen, and that often what is not seen is more important. Besides influencing John Paul II, it also did, among others, the Jewish Carmelite nun Edith Stein, who was murdered in Auschwitz, and thinkers as opposed to the former as Jean-Paul Sartre.

They asked a person who swept the floor in Cape Canaveral what he did, and he said: "Go to the Moon," and he was right, because the details are more important than it seems.

There are many important things that are not visible

In the vast majority of cases, innovation is not about addressing major transformation projects, doing spectacular things, but about working on improving our day-to-day life. Waiting to make major changes is an easy excuse, but if we forget the details, we will never find the time to fix minor flaws.

Avoiding discontinuities

In the history of mankind, there have been significant technological stoppages, which are unjustifiable in processes of continuous innovation. Right now, we are stumbling over the same stone a second time, that is, we were already wrong once: it is about the nuclear outage. Nuclear power is certainly a very complex technology that is not without dangers, but it is also a very important source of clean energy. We are now halfway, since we do not have a sufficiently consolidated solution. We are extending the life of first- and second-generation plants, which were designed in 1950 and, therefore, clearly improvable. The cycle of improvement was first broken following the tragedy of Chernobyl due to reckless endangerment. Now, we are about to repeat it, because of the accident of

Fukushima, this time owing to the uncontrollable forces of nature. They are two very different accidents with different consequences and, in the second case, highly magnified; suffice it to compare the thirty thousand deaths directly caused by the earthquake and subsequent tsunami to the ones caused by the hydrogen explosions at the Fukushima reactors; no casualties, officially. Has anyone counted the deaths by silicosis caused each year by coal mines or the CO_2 released into the atmosphere by plants consuming it?

Obviously, the safety of nuclear power plants may be improved, especially in the processes of stopping their reaction owing to natural disasters. We should not forget that the Chernobyl accident was due to an incorrect action that can only be understood on the basis of an obsolete political system, which was decaying and acting desperately. The explosion at Chernobyl, as far as I gathered at the time, when I worked at Asco Nuclear Power Plant in Tarragona, was due to reactor core overheating. It seems that the operators were exploring how to start up the plant without external power supply and, therefore, raised all granite bars that control the nuclear reaction; within milliseconds, they lost control, and everything ended up terribly. Soviet plants, unlike Western ones, tend not to shutdown themselves. What cannot be discussed, in any case, is that nuclear power is not only able to generate a lot of electricity, but also provides some energy independence to Western countries; thus, giving up this source, as has been done in some countries, without even a thorough debate and stopping research in this field, is pure recklessness. The logic thing to do is to develop third-generation plants, replacing old with new ones, and strengthen research in the field of nuclear fusion until we manage to replace nuclear fission power plants.

Another example, which is not as dramatic, is the case of the commercial Concorde jet aircraft. If the technology to cross the Atlantic in two hours exists, why do we do it in eight? The Concorde, such as nuclear power plants, was designed many years ago; now we would certainly do it better, with less environmental impact; we are repeating the mistake of breaking the virtuous circle of innovation, the continuous improvement cycle. The software industry is clear about it: it accepts that programs can always be improved, that they even have flaws, and continually releases new versions and updates.

Part II

OBSTACLES AND BARRIERS

5. Mental laziness

People only actually change when
they realize the consequences of not doing so.
Mario Alonso Puig

Why is it so hard to change? Man is a creature of repetition. He or she acquires virtues by repeating good deeds and accumulates vices with repeated wrongdoing. The same happens with organizations of any kind. Resistance to change is one of the most studied aspects of psychology as well as by organizational experts. Since I am passionate about this topic, I have read quite a few books and thought a lot about it. We all have our comfort zone, and any change jeopardizes it; thus, it is easier not to change, not to innovate, to be carried along by habits. That attitude, when taken to the extreme, becomes "hello laziness."

We all hope to get struck by lightning one day for life to change us automatically and effortlessly, as we think happened to Saul of Tarsus[21]. But this does not happen, nor is it likely that it happened to Saint Paul. Since what is not explained and merely discussed by scholars, as they can gather from the explanation given by the affected himself in his letter to the Galatians[22], is that Paul most likely retired for three years in Arabia after his fall. According to these sources, there, Saul must

---

[21] Acts of the Apostles, 9, 1-30.

[22] Galatians 11-18.

have engaged in study and meditation and in preparing properly for his new mission. The change in activity of Saul, now called Paul, was not an instantaneous event. Like Saul, in our life an extraordinary event may befall us that acts as a trigger for change, but for this to confirm, you will have to work on it and need to overcome a period of adaptation and learning.

In his book, *Vivir es una necesidad urgente* (Living is an urgent need), Mario Alonso Puig says: "People only actually change when they realize the consequences of not doing so." This consideration also applies to any type of organization. We must be alert so as not to be late when detecting that a change was necessary. Quitting smoking when you are diagnosed with cancer is worse than if you had done it before, maybe we could have prevented it.

"The party is over" is the famous headline that *The Economist* published on November 11, 2008[23], to refer to the bursting of the housing bubble in Spain and means just that. It is over indeed, bringing about an unemployment rate close to 27% and general confusion. If we do not realize now that we should make changes, when we are already enduring the consequences, I do not know when we are going to.

Being critical

Laziness is always a mental thing. To think is hard and tiring. We do not think much, and if you do not

---

[23] www.slideshare.net/rgonzalop/the-economist-spain-special-report-the-partys-over

think, you do not realize the consequences of your deeds. Thus, we remain in the comfort zone, which is actually a false comfort. From the reflections by the philosopher José Antonio Marina, I gather that mental laziness has two distinct justifications; firstly, that of fanatics and, secondly, that of skeptics. The former are so sure of their ideas that they do not even think of questioning them, whereas the latter say it is not worth questioning them, because improvement is impossible. Following Marina's classification, the third type, the critic, is the one that wonders, searches, and believes that through analysis, experimentation, and deduction progress, getting closer to the truth is possible. Let us promote the need for analysis and criticism.

We have already mentioned that excessive entertainment, being distracted with anything, avoids thinking and prevents reflection. If we looked at it from a revolutionary perspective, the powerful are interested in promoting entertainment, in organizing circuses. They tell us to get comfortable and not to worry about anything, that Daddy/Nanny State will take care of us and that we will not lack anything.

6. The players

Find out who you are gambling with.

Marina's classification into types has also been addressed by other authors and from other aspects. Three types of people are mentioned. Firstly, the change agents, who are people that make things happen; secondly, those who observe how things happen; and, thirdly, people that are amazed that something happened, especially if change was for the better. My American colleague, Janet Smith, an independent telecommunications consultant, explained in her presentations that, when addressing a project, you must always identify the players and propose to classify them as friends, enemies, or neutral; I was surprised by Smith's presentation with regard to how naturally she addressed the issue, in a very realistic American way, by calling things by their name. If the features of the team's players are recognized, you can try to make the most of them. Do not assume that everyone has the right attitude, because this is not the case. Nor is it usual that they have the necessary skills, the knowledge they should boast or that is required. However, with the right attitude it is always much easier to acquire the necessary skills.

I like to talk about constructive, destructive, and vegetative attitudes. Vegetative attitudes should be less frequent, as they are not typical of a rational animal like human beings, but, in my opinion, they are the most common ones. A vegetative attitude chooses comfort and thinks: "I better not take a risk, let someone else make decisions, I should not bother, lest they tell me that I throw cogs in the wheels and I expose myself, if the project eventually turns out well." What characterizes a vegetable is that it is planted, that is, immobile. Being present, an attitude that reminds me of burials with the body present, those in which the coffin containing the body of the deceased is present during the ceremony, and it is there, because someone has put it there, it is obvious that he or she has not shown up by themselves at their own funeral.

Wisdom contained in the Bible also teaches us and confirms that the skeptical, indifferent, vegetative attitude is the most dangerous one. For example, even Revelation, the last book of the New Testament which was written by Saint John the Evangelist, Jesus' favorite disciple, prevents us from such attitudes; the letter of the angel of the church in Laodicea reads: "I know your deeds, that you are neither cold nor hot. I wish you were either one or the other! So, because you are lukewarm—neither hot nor cold—I am about to spit you out of my mouth."[24] A tough message that the angel conveys to the Church of Laodicea in God's name. Luckily, the angel says *I am about to spit you* and not *I will spit you,* as is sometimes stated, which indicates that we can always hope for God's mercy and, instead of encountering a condemnation, we must realize that we are facing a call to change that we should not let drop into oblivion. We must be alert, as the last verse of the letter reminds us: "He who has an

---

[24] Revelation 3, 15-16.

ear, let him hear what the Spirit says to the churches." Lukewarmness can also be called mediocrity. By the way, Revelation is not the doomsday book, but the one that foretells a new era, which is better than the current one. Some authors even suggest that Revelation suggests a continuous conversion.[25]

Mario Alonso Puig even speaks about "black hole" people and advises not to get too close to them, lest they gobble you down. They would be like an energy sink.

A management cliché they teach at business schools is that you have to surround yourself with the best people, that you have to have the best team. The importance of good staff recruitment is obvious, which is a very difficult task, especially because neither the necessary time nor resources are dedicated to it; on the contrary, it is common to act hastily in this regard. In many cases, incorporating the best people into our team is not possible, either because of their cost or because they are not available. It also happens that the people we categorize as the best are actually not, because the truth is that you never know how people will respond to certain situations or how a project will unfold, and, ultimately, what the future has in store for us. The person who was optimal or ideal for launching the

> Surround yourself with the best people is impossible

---

[25] "Paschal" interpretation model of Revelation, quoted by Ignacio Rojas in *Qué se sabe de... Los símbolos del Apocalipsis,* Verbo Divino, 2013 (What is known about ... The symbols of Revelation).

> Lead a team is get that each of the members gives the best of themselves

project may not be so at later stages. Moreover, the political, economic, social, technological, and environmental circumstances change. Meanwhile, people also evolve, should mature and grow in knowledge and wisdom, but it is not always like that. In addition, any company or project needs different profiles, and it is no use to have highly trained people performing lower-skilled jobs, as they will become frustrated. Therefore, I think it is smart to not surround yourself with the best—which I think is impossible—, but to make the most of each of the team members and for the entire group to evolve better in a virtuous circle of growth. Team components can and should improve continuously and be permanently trained or learning. I think the concept of *learning organization* is very accurate.

Another major cliché is that we cannot change and, therefore, categorize people in a hurry. Change can be difficult or very difficult, but by no means impossible. We have already quoted Mario Alonso Puig: "People only actually change when they realize the consequences of not doing so." Therefore, what is really an exciting challenge, and even more so for a business leader or project manager, is to get a team to acquire the appropriate attitude for the necessary changes to take place. The collaborators will accept a new procedure by themselves and receive proper training to get the precise skills, if we manage that they have the right attitude.

Neutral or vegetative attitudes actually hide negative attitudes, are hidden enemies. Zero growth is a fallacy: either you row or you are a drag, a dead weight that keeps the canoe from advancing or the balloon from rising. Staying in a company for fifteen years without doing anything[26], neither

> A real leader gets that the team acquire the appropriate attitude

good nor bad, is stealing, even if it happens by omission and even if the company allows it, or does not know how to avoid it, or worse, even though detecting it, does not have the legal or economic tools to prevent it.

In reality, you should not label people. No one is one hundred percent one way or another nor always behaves the same, but the classifications mentioned are approximations that are very close to reality and help us to know whom we are playing with and how to get the most out of each person in the team. The more constructive people we have, the better results we get. The fewer destroyers there are, the less there will be to rebuild. Even if you are not the team leader, a positive and constructive attitude always contributes something. Parents, educators, business leaders, heads of department, or project managers should imbue their children, students, and collaborators with a constructive attitude.

Who plays the game of innovation in an organization? Well, everyone, the whole organization, from

---

[26] Example: Hello laziness.

top management to human resources, through marketing, finance, sales, production, and, above all, organization and systems. Furthermore, we will have to hire external players, such as consultants, vendors, integrators, and installers. The attitudes we have mentioned should not only be individual, but also collective in nature: they have to be shared by entire departments or groups of people. In that sense, we must be alert for negative group dynamics, of the sort *the mediocre people united will never be defeated.* Mediocrity networks are very difficult to undo and are usually transversal. That is to say, we may not only find a cyst of mediocrity, but a whole network that is distributed over different levels and departments of the organization. Mediocrity triumphs in dormant, anesthetized, apathetic, or demoralized societies.

In any case, it is important to identify the focus of all players, since we will have at least the opportunity to manage the situation and change it, if we know and accept the team's limitations. If you think that everyone will collaborate spontaneously, there will be more difficulties. It is a mistake of a utopian nature to expect that there will be a perfect team to address an innovation or improvement process; you must do it with the available team, getting the most out of it.

Similarly to the transversal nature of mediocrity, intractable people, on the one end, and constructive ones, at the other end, are distributed likewise. In all teams and at all levels, there are always people who will bring values and who want to build. The smart thing is to discover and rely on them. After all, it is about detecting natural leaders and get the key people in the organization to take the lead.

7. Envy

*Envy is behind
lose-lose agreements.*

I have decided to dedicate a chapter to this subject, because I have seen the great destructive power of this deadly sin. I have found that many decisions are taken under its influence and none should be taken in this sorry state.

The deadly sins, seven, were stated by Pope Gregory the Great in the 6th century and widely studied by Saint Thomas Aquinas. These vices are described as "capital," because they are considered the source of many other sins, that is to say, they are a source of misfortune. The virtue that opposes envy is charity, which is the great virtue. *Deus caritas est*[27] is the first encyclical letter of Pope Benedict XVI. "God is charity: God is love. Charity is to always wish and do good to others. That to confront envy we have to employ charity gives us an idea of how dangerous this matter is.

José Antonio Marina[28] considers envy a passion. And passion is defined as "intense, vehement, biased feelings that are exerting a powerful influence on

---

[27] www.vatican.va/holy_father/benedict_xvi/encyclicals/documents/ hf_ben-xvi_enc_20051225_deus-caritas-est_sp.html

[28] Marina features a very broad and interesting literature on these issues, which was published by the Anagrama publishing house.

the individual." It is indeed a destructive feeling that many people find difficult to manage; unfortunately, it is usual to bump into people dominated by it. This matter is so serious that it already appears in the first book of the Bible, Genesis, the same that explains creation. Cain killed his brother Abel out of envy[29].

Envy is an intrinsic feature of the destroyer. The envious person thinks that, if an idea is not theirs, it should not succeed, because someone else will claim the medal and, if the case is significant, a rebalancing of internal power will occur, which will surely harm them. The Spanish Royal Academy[30] defines envy as a sadness or sorrow for another's goods, but what is extraordinary is that people get to prefer the evil of all instead of recognizing a third party's achievements. In fact, Napoleon already said that envy is a declaration of inferiority. Envy is a very Hispanic feature. Jorge Luis Borges said: "The issue of envy is very Spanish. Spanish people are always thinking about envy. If they want to state that something is good, they say: "It is enviable." It is amazing how the language we use describes us! Neurolinguists have a great future. In this sense, the already quoted José Antonio Marina has worked extensively on the meaning and use of words to analyze the character of a society. If Borges is right, and I think he is, we face a maze of mediocrity, that is, Borges already knew what the survey revealed in the book *Alerta y desconfianza. La sociedad española ante la crisis*. (Alert and distrust. The Spanish society before the crisis).

---

[29] Genesis 4.

[30] lema.rae.es/drae/?val=envidia

Doubtlessly, envy is behind lose-lose agreements: "He shall be neither mine nor yours; divide him."[31] This is the terrible sentence uttered by the woman who tried to steal a baby, as told in the Bible. King Solomon, who was renowned for his wisdom, resolves the dispute over the maternity of a child causing a lose-lose deal: "Divide the living child in two, and give half to the one and half to the other." The real mother's waiver of the agreement and the fake mother's acceptance of the same allow the king to solve the problem. The fake mother, dominated by envy, prefers death of yet another child. Hers had died, and she could not bear the happiness of the other mother, so she does not mind that everybody loses: If I cannot have mine, neither shall you have yours.

Let us go to war and break everything. Many of our politicians think: Since I am not in command, the worse, the better. That is how we are doing: Instead of learning from history, we persist in repeating it. We cannot work while ignoring this issue. We have to prevent it from entering a project, an organization. Discretion is a good strategy for dealing with destructive envy and mediocrity. We recommend not to awaken it, not to cause it. Any suggestion on how, if not to avoid it, at least manage it will be well received, because this matter is a major barrier and, therefore, constitutes a major challenge to overcome it.

We need more cooperation and less competition, less envy and more admiration for the success and contribution of others, which we hope they know how to share.

---

[31] I Kings 3, 26.

8.   Procrastination

Do not do today what
you can leave for tomorrow.
Instead, focus on what must be done
today, and it will have more impact.
Phil Edholm

Procrastinating is an ugly verb which is hard to pro-
nounce, but is very easy to implement. Procrastinating
means delaying decisions. Never finding the right
time to do something. It is very easy to get a lot of
arguments for not taking a decision. Drs. Jane B. Burka
and Leonora M. Yuen have extensively studied this
phenomenon and summarized their knowledge in the
book *Procrastination. Why you do it, what to do about
it Now* . I found, and bought, the revised and updated
edition, which was published to mark the twenty-fifth
anniversary of the first edition, on the bestseller shelf
of the Massachusetts Institute of Technology book-
store in Boston. I think it was no accident to find that
book where I found it. It is quite interesting that, in
a polytechnic college, which is highly acclaimed and
boasts an international reputation for research and
innovation, this topic is a matter of concern. Perhaps
it is because they know the human condition all too
well, as it is a very human flaw that affects all societies. Thus, without a doubt, the smartest thing to do
is to recognize the phenomenon, study its causes, and
know how we can act to overcome it.

Procrastinating is a widespread habit: The age of marriage is delayed, as well as the age to have a child, to stop smoking, to exercise more and also the moment to tackle a new project, to learn another language, etc. We must remember that omission is not the correct action, as it means to stop doing one thing we should have done. There is the sin of omission, as there is also the duty to help. Sins, in general, are not fashionable, but that of omission seems to have disappeared off the face of the Earth, when, in my opinion, it is the most common one. That of omission is, therefore, a discreet and demure sin.

There are thousands of excuses for inaction, I dare to list some of them:

- We have no budget.
- I do not control anything.
- We are not independent.
- We have no team.
- We are not organized.
- We do not know enough.
- We have to think it over more.
- It will be for nothing. There is no need.

Some of them, or even several, may be true, but this can also be viewed from another perspective:

Given the lack of economic resources, which is very common, we can thoroughly analyze the costs or look for other models that differ from traditional ones, such as pay per use.

Power, actual, real power, well, is held by a tiny minority, but not exercising power does not mean that you cannot have authority, and there is always steerability. Influencing is achieved not by remaining silent, but by suggesting ideas and exposing inefficiencies.

Nobody boasts full independence and freedom of action. Most regions of the world do not have an independent state; in fact, the most prosperous ones are not independent (New York, California, Bavaria, Piedmont, Veneto). They do have a high degree of autonomy, but true wealth is generated by business and not by control over state structures, most of which are obsolete.

Teams are set up and must be multidisciplinary and include people outside the organization. Project work, in which results are rewarded, fares better. You should not be paid for going to work, for being there, but for the work done.

To be properly organized is a matter of being willing to do so.

Nobody knows everything, but it is okay to ask people who know and ask others for help.

Excess analysis reveals too many difficulties and generates a certain blocking trend. Analyses must be balanced and dispassionate.

Nihilism, denying the significance of our actions, makes no sense. It is a self-fulfilling prophecy. If we believe that we are not going to make it, we will actually not do anything.

However, warning against procrastination does not suggest precipitation in any way. Success is, as Frankl explains, what is done during the time period that elapses from the moment the impulse to act is received until you act. Thinking and dominating our reaction.

My colleague, Phil Edholm, proposes in his book, *Napkin Logic. 48 Great Business Ideas, Lessons, and Rules, and Insights to make you a better business person and entrepreneur,* to refine the saying "Do not leave for tomorrow what you can do today" and transform it into the quote that heads this chapter: "Do not do today what can wait until tomorrow; you better focus on what must be done today, and it will have a greater impact," that is to say, you have to prioritize, implement first things first.

For Stephen Covey, putting first things first is the third habit of a highly effective person, as reflected in his book, *First things first,* a guide to manage time. In my case, I try to implement his recommendations by going over my to-do list of the previous day every morning before I start my workday, crossing out the completed tasks and adding new ones, as they arise in my mind; then I take the red pen and prioritize them. It is not a great method, but it works.

To complete the comments on this subject I cannot help quoting Mother Teresa of Calcutta, founder of the Missionaries of Charity: "There should be less talk; a preaching point is not a meeting point. What do you do then? Take a broom and clean someone's house. That says enough." My free interpretation of this reflection, adapted to the world of business or to oneself, is that, on the one hand, we must turn things around less, hold fewer meetings, and appoint less coordinators and, on the other, we must lead more and act more[32], because, otherwise, our homes are being left unswept.

We must find the balance between Martha and Mary, Lazarus' sisters, whom Jesus resurrected. Con-

---

[32] A coordinator and a manager are not the same.

templation and action[33]: The Gospel praises Martha, but few remember that, if everyone had remained contemplating Jesus, nobody would have eaten

Ora et labora

there. *Ora et labora* says the Rule of Saint Benedict of Nursia[34] (4th century). Modern translation into everyday life is: reflect and act. In fact, reflection requesting the inspiration of the Holy Spirit is prayer.

---

[33] Luke 10, 38-42.

[34] www.osb.org

9. Commitment phobia

A diamond is forever.

My office is located in a major shopping area of Barcelona, the most frequented by tourists. Since I have settled down here, over twenty years ago, the commercial offer has changed. One change that my wife has mademe realize is that several jewelry stores are gone, which, interestingly, have been replaced by low-cost lingerie stores. There has been a decline in the gift offer, an unequivocal sign of a long-term commitment, often for life, and which passes from mother to daughter, from grandmother to granddaughter, of what constitutes "a diamond is forever", and, instead, there has been an increase in the supply of signs of immediate, fast, and fleeting pleasure. I am not saying that there should not be this offer nor do I advocate for puritanism, but I found it a curious effect and appropriate to introduce this chapter. I guess I see here an example of the growing fear of commitment. Certainly, giving lingerie commits you much less, however expensive and fine it is, than offering a diamond; it especially commits much less the pocket of the giving person.

It is hard to commit oneself. We notice a fear to compromise. There is a clear tendency not to take risks, much like Pontius Pilate. It is hard to defend a position. It is not easy to find out what someone thinks about a particular subject.

Another example is the mother who tells her daughter to marry in a civil ceremony and not in a church, because this way she is committing less. It is assumed that it will end badly. With this approach, there are actually more chances that the union will not prosper. I am not talking about religious beliefs here, but about the strength of commitment, of the will to succeed: failure is predicted and, therefore, it is encouraged that this materializes.

Today, in Europe, the number of births outside of formal marriages reaches 39.3%[35] of the total figure. I ponder: If many of our fellow citizens see no need to commit by signing a marriage contract even when they decide to have biological offspring[36], how much harder will it get for them to engage in other projects.

On the other hand, I think the American practice of giving a plaque, which reads: "Thank you for your commitment", to those people you want to honor and thank for the services rendered is quite right. It is a sign that their commitment is valued, that this factor is considered essential to the success of a company. Recognizing the dedication, interest, initiative, and contributions of a person is a good practice. We should congratulate and thank on many more occasions than we actually do.

---

[35] According to the Report on the evolution of the family in Spain, which was published in 2014 and drafted by the Spanish Institute for Family Policy from data of the National Institute of Statistics and Eurostat. In Spain, the figure is 38.9%.

[36] Having a child is a long-term project shared by two people. In its traditional way, a man and a woman, father and mother. That is to say, it is the work of a complementary team which takes, at least, eighteen years, until the child comes of age.

I consider the definition of commitment as a contracted obligation as incomplete. There is more to commitment, it is a will, a promise, a hope, a strong belief that you want to achieve a goal and that all means at your disposal will be made available to achieve it.

A highly committed and excited team greatly contributed to the success of the 1992 Olympic Games. Few people left the team, and this in spite of the fact that the subsequent crisis could be discerned and that people were facing unemployment, as it actually happened. Some colleagues took over a year to relocate and others returned to their previous companies, although they had sworn they would not. After the Games, our phone did not ring for months, nobody called us. Just the opposite of when we were organizing and running the Games, when everybody was calling us and the phone never stopped ringing.

The problem of a commitment-phobic person lies in a misconception of the concept of freedom, as explained by the philosopher and Catholic priest, Joan Martínez Porcell, former dean of the Ecclesiastical Faculty of Philosophy of Catalonia[37], who explains that the trend has spread that "we are freer the less things we decide on. Thus, it seems that being free means not to be committed to anything or anyone." As we have already discussed, the pair freedom/responsibility is broken. We are truly free when we are able to bear the consequences of the actions we choose.

---

[37] www.joanmp.es

People suffering from Peter Pan syndrome, who are permanent adolescents, are the top-ten candidates among commitment-phobic people.

Commitment phobia is not only a wrong attitude; it is, above all, a generator of poverty. You cannot build a medium- or long-term project without commitment; actually, not even on a short term.

10. Conformity

Blessed Mary, blessed Mary,
let me remain like I am today.

The light at the end of the tunnel
might be a train.

"Blessed Mary, blessed Mary, let me remain like I am today"[38] is a sentence that is heard too often. Furthermore, in my very humble opinion, it could even be a theological aberration in it Spanish version. What is really appropriate is what Saint Augustine recommends: "Pray as if everything depended on God and work as if everything depended on you;" this way we are indeed likely to succeed. Another version of the same positive recommendation is "God helps those who help themselves." Being content with the given situation is moving back. I am very satisfied with the car I have, that is perfect, but surely nobody thinks that he or she will never change it.

We aim to seek security and stability, which, in practice, neither exist nor nobody and nothing can provide us with. That does not mean that you should not be cautious and keep your grain if you have had

---

[38] This is a Spanish expression. "The light at the end of the tunnel might be a train" could be an English proverb that express similar ideas.

a good harvest. It does not mean to be reckless or a brainless person, but you do have to be very aware that the future must be earned day by day; there will surely be unexpected events, imperfections, doubts, disappointments, but they should not prevent us from acting.

Lack of rebellion, of positive stress, of nonconformity is a disaster in itself. As Martínez Porcell says, we are unfinished and have, thus, the opportunity to build ourselves. Why do we resign? How many people think they have to be content with everything! Of course, you have to appreciate more what you have than what you do not have, the good rather than the bad, and accept what cannot be changed, but without courage to act, to change what does have to be modified, we will do worse each time.

You cannot be a *peix bullit* (boiled fish), a graphic Catalan expression to identify bland, passive, amorphous people. That is, you cannot go through life without any taste.

The call to nonconformity and rebellion does not mean to promote rupture or a bloody revolution, but a call to accept reality, to finish the unfinished, and to improve the imperfect, even if we know that perfection is unattainable and perfectionism is insane. But improvement is within our reach indeed. And, best of all, as it has no limit, it is never going to end. Continuous evolution versus revolution.

Undoubtedly, the Serenity Prayer is wonderful and very realistic. As I was unable to determine its origin with certainty (Saint Augustine or Saint Francis of Assisi, or perhaps it was inspired by the wise Roman emperor Marcus Aurelius or the evangelical pastor

Reinhold Niebuhr), I do not dare attributing it to anyone:

*God, grant me the serenity to accept the things
I cannot change, the courage to change the things
I can and the wisdom to know the difference.*

11. The communication gap

A gap is an empty space,
a great distance between two people.

Call him,
or rather video call him.

Human communication is very complicated. A lot of times we say A, when we really mean B, plus our interlocutor understands C[39]. Human communication is influenced by many factors, from cultural and linguistic to psychological and biological ones.

Customizing the message

Compared to telecommunications, we can say that, for a recipient to understand the message from a sender, the two should be in sync, that is, broadcast and receive on the same frequency. We cannot send a message on a different channel than the one the recipient is tuning in, because they will not receive it. The sender must adapt their message to the recipient.

A typical example is when a technician presents an idea, a project, or a concept to others who lack

---

[39] The book by John Gray, *Men Are from Mars, Women Are from Venus*, in which he addresses the communication difficulties between men and women, is interesting, entertaining, and even funny.

adequate technical training or knowledge of the terminology being used. Communication difficulties between the information technologies and communications departments (ICT) and the other departments within the organization, including senior management, are obvious. For the proposals of a department or technician to be welcomed by their peers, the experts have to improve their communication, as they cannot expect the CEO to learn certain concepts (eventually, they will seek advice from their teenage son).

My friend and colleague, John Purnell III[40], in order to avoid using technical terms in his conferences, uses the following trick: When starting his papers, he deposits a pile of ten-dollar bills on the table and gives one to each attendee who catches him uttering a mnemonic such as VLAN, MPLS, IP, UC2, SIP, or others, instead of explaining the concept. Each conference costs John a few dollars; in return, he manages, thus, that his attendees are never distracted.

Therefore, every message we want to communicate must be built very well, it must be in line with the objective sought and adapted to those who, in each particular case, are going to be the recipients.

Persuasion channels

Neurolinguists teach us that human beings have three channels of persuasion: auditory, visual, and kines-

---

[40] www.inspireddatasolutions.com

thetic (touch) and point out that the most important one is the visual channel. The Brazilian neurolinguist Lair Ribeiro graphically expresses this by assigning a percentage to each of these channels; 12% to the kinesthetic, 35% to the auditory, and an overwhelming 53% to the visual channel.

Bandwidth and communication quality

In electronic communications, there is a direct relationship between bandwidth and communication quality. The bandwidth measures the transmission capacity, how much information can be transmitted at a given time; it is equivalent to the diameter of a pipe, the larger it is, the bigger the flow it holds. Thus, a text message via mobile phone (SMS), email, or chat is a narrowband communication, that is, a small pipe is enough. By contrast, a telepresence meeting, with a life-size video, is a broadband communication and needs much more capacity.

Email dangers

Narrowband communications (mobile SMS messages, chats, instant messaging, and email) are inherently poor, as they contain very little information and often use a sign language, which is unknown to many people, their own slang coined by a digital generation; ultimately, they are very prone to misunderstandings.

Emails are very dangerous and are badly used. The main problems are as follows:

- They are poorly written. Writing well is not easy, takes time, and you have to reread what you have written. Never forget that, as Pontius Pilate said, "What I have written, I have written."
- They are sent to too many people, many of which are not directly affected by the matter and often have no time to read all the emails they get.
- It is too easy to forward an email, and you cannot control where it ends. Many end up where they should not be.
- Internal communications are forwarded to external people, sometimes with inappropriate comments.

My partner, Luis Pernas, a skilled observer, remarked to me one day how the broadcast effect, or mass distribution of emails, with a copy to superiors, was a factor that was generating delays (procrastinator) and a very useful tool for commitment-phobic people. "As I have already informed my boss, he should take risks now." Decisions are made at increasingly higher levels of the organization: as keeping the boss informed is so easy, everything goes up. Thus, the management is saturated, and a vicious circle is established. To the already difficult task of delegating the ease with which partners get rid of a problem by passing it on to the upper level is added. Thus, many ineffective intermediate layers are created that act as a transmission belt, which are unable to decide, nor willing to do so, and do nothing to improve the organization.

In the army, there is the so-called "official channel," which consists in that developments are passed on to the immediate superior, and you cannot skip a level and inform others that are above them. When I was part of the Spanish Air Force for eighteen months, I did not like this way of acting, but over time I have come to the conclusion that it was not that badly devised. Skipping official channels should be an exception, not the rule to unlock issues.

Calling by phone

We are abusing email and instant messaging. People protect themselves behind a screen and a keyboard. What a shame! I reclaim phone calls, which show a clear regression. We are calling less and less and we forget that in a telephone conversation much more information is conveyed than in an email, because the intonation, voice modulation, and direct interaction provide a wealth of nuances. As important as what is said, or even more so, is how it is said.

On the other hand, I do not advise abusing conference calls. Phone meetings with several participants are a mess. Moreover, if there are several people in a room using a hands-free phone, no one will understand clearly what is being said; as the interlocutors are not seen, several attendees use the moment to do something else. In some cases, participation of a person is only detected because they are on the list of attendees included in the minutes. We should abolish conference calls[41] once and for all and replace them with video conferencing.

---

[41] The above happens as you can see in this video: http://youtu.be/DYubGbZiiQ

Those working in television are well aware of the fact that humans are tolerant as regards poor video quality, but quite intolerant in terms of bad audio quality.

Video calls

Better than a phone call is to conduct a video conference. Seeing the face of the interlocutor provides a differential factor: How much information is reflected on the face, the mirror of our soul! By phone it is easi-

> The face
> is the mirror
> of the soul

er to lie (let alone in a chat). Why then do we insist on giving it up? And that happens, even if John Chambers, president of Cisco Systems, already said a few years ago in his paper at the Barcelona Mobile World Congress that "the world is moving towards visual communication." The reality is that it is moving much slower than it seems. People are reserved as to showing you their face in a video conference. I know of one company that has implemented a customer service video center; Bankinter, a traditional bank, which really opted for new technologies and remains a pioneer in this field.

What communication channel to use

My colleague, Phil Edholm[42], has studied what the most appropriate channel is at all times of a business

---

[42] www.pkeconsulting.com

relationship. I had the opportunity to attend his presentation, "Concepts for the future of real-time collaboration," during the Conference of the Society of Communications Technology Consultants[43] in Orlando in October 2011, and I consider it very fruitful to analyze some of the ideas he presented. Edholm distinguishes various channels and classifies them according to the richness of interaction; ordered from highest (1) to lowest (8), they are as follows:

1. Face-to-face meeting.
2. Video conference with collaboration tools that allow you to share documents and board in real time.
3. Video conferencing.
4. Phones with collaboration tools.
5. Telephony.
6. Instant messaging (chat).
7. Email.
8. Voice message.

On this scale, he traces two lines, hence separating the visual channels (1 to 3), the real-time channels (1 to 6), and the asynchronous channels (7 and 8).

Depending on the degree of familiarity or knowledge between the partners and their culture (West and East are not the same), he considers it acceptable or unacceptable to use a particular channel. Moreover, he recommends appropriate channels to carry out a sales process or consolidation of a relationship and appropriate channels for the development of a project. It is funny how he completely discourages you to email during a sales process.

---

[43] www.sctcconsultants.org

Obtaining and retaining the attention of the receiver

Furthermore, Edholm introduces in his analysis another interesting concept, that of attention management, which refers to how to get your partners to pay attention to what the sender is transmitting. In a meeting, and even more so in a presentation, it is very difficult that attendees are not distracted. There are too many temptations, the mobile phone does not stop receiving messages, and many people are anxious to read them and reply immediately. Attention management in any type of communication is an art. You have to not just select the appropriate channel and build the message contents to be able to retain the attention; you must especially impact, convince, seduce.

I remember the first time I gave a presentation at a conference in the US, my mentor, Henry Baird, suggested that I place the transparency I reserved for the end, as a summary and conclusion, at the beginning of my presentation. He made me see that the first thing you say is most important: you need to attract attention, make a good first impression, and then keep up the rhythm. There is only a single chance to make a good first impression.

The relevance of communication

Communicating well is essential to the success of any company. It is a very difficult challenge, which you never control completely, because we must always strive to improve communication. For that purpose, you need to practice; like most things, you learn based on hours and repeating. In Spain, you are not taught how to communicate, discuss, argue, which is, therefore, a training gap we need to overcome. You have to read

> There is only a single chance to make a good first impression

books on the subject, participate in seminars. We must complete the training we have received, not use its shortcomings as an excuse. If we were not able or did not want to study at the time, we still have time to do so.

The key point to good communication is the ability to empathize, that is to say, to put yourself in the place of another. If we know what concerns them, where it hurts them, what motivates them, and what goals they have, we can adapt our message to the interlocutor.

> The key point to good communication is the ability to empathize

While this book is not about communication, seeing that it is one of the major shortcomings, especially in highly skilled technical people, makes it convenient to talk about it. In summary, here are some tips for improving communication:

1. Reading books; helps improve the richness of vocabulary and grammatical constructions. You learn to write by reading.
2. Selecting the appropriate channel for each communication, prioritizing phone calls over email,

and video calls over voice-only calls. Using the maximum bandwidth available.

3. As much as possible, maintaining personal, one-to-one meetings.

4. Establishing a personal relationship takes time. For that, we must devote time to being with other people, mostly on a one-to-one basis or in small groups. Lunches, breakfasts, coffees, beers, or travels are opportunities that, undoubtedly, help to strengthen a relationship. Regular contact brings affection.

5. Showing your face, stating your views at meetings, not shutting up. Preparing your contributions well.

6. Email should not be used to change your mind or to point out what you have been unable to propose or defend in a physical meeting.

7. Some news has to be digested. You have to communicate it, as much as possible, gradually. If a plane crashes and there are no survivors, someone has to break the news in all its rawness, but if it is a terminal illness, you can prepare the family in a gradual manner. The same applies to a company. Do not give bad news by email.

8. Using the language and channel of our partner, as he should feel comfortable, not us. The sender should do the effort, not the recipient of the message.

9. Adapting our language to the comprehension skills of our interlocutors.

10. Using examples and understandable stories to reinforce the message. The best communicator in history is Jesus of Nazareth, he spoke in parables.

Part III

STRATEGIES AND TOOLS

12. What kind of tools do we have?

*Never has mankind
had so many
tools available.*

With this chapter, we are introducing the third section of the book. In the first one, we have mentioned the environment in which we operate; in the second one, some of the barriers and obstacles we encounter were discussed, and now we wonder: what can we do and what resources do we have?

I doubt if my explanation up to this point has been exceedingly pessimistic. This is not at all my intention, but we cannot evade the situation we are living in and the environment around us. Part of the Western world is undergoing a deep crisis, which is economic, institutional, and apparently deconstructing the so-called "welfare state," which, in my opinion, it was not; it had dangerously degenerated towards a vegetating state. In any case, we have focused on building a comfort zone that is unreal. Welfare does not mean to have it all sorted out and tick over. True welfare means being satisfied with oneself. To be satisfied with oneself, you have to contribute, you must help others. John Fitzgerald

> True welfare means being satisfied with oneself

> Ask not what your country can do for you, ask what you can do for your country
>
> *JFK*

Kennedy was totally right when he said: "Ask not what your country can do for you, ask what you can do for your country." That idea is equally valid when applied to the family, city, community, region, or humankind.

Therefore, the real crisis, the most worrying one, is the crisis of values and attitudes.

Change is for the better

It is indisputable that many things are changing very quickly, but that does not mean that the planet is going to disappear. Evolution will not stop; even with its ups and downs, it is indisputable that we are moving toward a better world than this one.

Humanity has experienced and overcome much more serious situations than the present one. Just a few decades ago, with the Second World War, Nazism and Communism and the subsequent Cold War, we were faring far worse. With the Cuban missile crisis, we almost destroyed ourselves.

Renewal

When a society, a company, or a person start to decline, it is because they have lost their values. The solution is simple: it consists in renewing oneself, while keeping the good things and removing the bad ones, all of which before such damage is irreversible. Renewal processes are a clear sign of the times we are living in. For example, an institution with more than two thousand years of history like the Catholic Church faces a major renewal under the charismatic leadership of Pope Francis. His predecessor, Benedict XVI, resigns in an unprecedented act to forcefully launch a renewal movement.

The good news

The good news is that we have many very good tools to renew ourselves and progress, the best tools humanity has ever had. Renewing oneself is popular.

We boast the best technology, great organizational skills, and strong philosophical grounds, which were developed over centuries, wisdom of all times.

In this third part of the book, we will reflect on various aspects regarding these three sets of tools. We are going to start at the base, the foundation; we will discuss the philosophical aspects first, then continue with the organizational ones, and finish with the technological tools; thus, we will move from most to least, from the most difficult things to implement in personal life or in an organization to the easiest.

Despite my engineering training and profession, I think installing a new technology in an organization is relatively easy; what is really complicated is the human factor, which needs, therefore, to be addressed first: before anything else, that which provides more value, even if it is the most difficult part.

Philosophy

Talking about philosophy is not popular. Neither studying it, as it has an increasingly marginal role in the curriculum, which is a blunder that can only be understood by the unspeakable desire of rulers to have servants and promote blind obedience, instead of educating citizens who are capable of growing and evolving.

There is no democracy without philosophy; both concepts were developed in ancient Greece. Philosophy teaches us to think, and this is the most important thing we have to teach our children and our teams.

I like to define philosophy as a body of knowledge that rationally seeks to establish the general principles organizing and guiding both the knowledge of reality and the meaning of human action. Philosophy, like psychology, sociology, logic, and related sciences, helps us to know ourselves.

With this definition in mind, I have grouped some basic tools, which are the roots. John Paul II, besides being a Pope, was a philosopher of the phenomenological school (already quoted above); he repeatedly stated that you cannot live without roots. In a company, its roots are its mission and corporate culture.

The "philosophical" concepts we are going to develop in the following chapters are:
- Attitudes and aptitudes (chapter 13).
- Hope (chapter 14).
- Proactivity and influence (chapter 15).
- Making decisions (chapter 16).

Organization

Moreover, based on some philosophical principles, human beings can organize themselves, design methodologies, procedures, practices, and rules that help us overcome or avoid our limitations and allow us to get the resources we need to survive and improve the material and spiritual welfare.

In the group of organizational tools, under a clear English influence, we will discuss best practices and lessons learned, which make sure that innovative projects are conducted properly and the expected results are ultimately achieved. Malpractices are also discussed, and we are advised of the risks they generate.

Getting organized means applying common sense, as so many things in life; a good knowledge of human nature, guarding against its flaws and limitations, while leaving ample room for maneuvers, with a fine degree of confidence in the team. Neither distrust everything nor stop worrying. A balance between supervision and autonomy.

The aspects we have classified as organizational include:
- The stool (chapter 17).
- External support (chapter 18).
- The analysis and strategy department (chapter 19).
- Selling innovation (chapter 20).
- Negotiation (chapter 21).
- Training and self-training (chapter 22).
- Meeting management (chapter 23).
- Project development (chapter 24).

- Crisis management (chapter 25).
- Leadership in innovation processes (chapter 26).

Technology

Humans also have a great ability to develop technological solutions in order to achieve, based on our scientific knowledge, practical applications thereof, which are used in industry, business, and our daily lives.

Technology is a powerful tool and a differential factor, as was demonstrated when we commented on the story of the Pomorska Brigade. Wars have almost always been won by those with the best technology. You cannot operate with outdated technologies or get entrenched in them, as they lead us to failure. If our competitors have better technology, their products will be more competitive than ours. Although technology should not be an end in itself, you should never underestimate its crucial importance.

As a specialist in communication technologies, in chapter 26 I will discuss briefly, the latest tools available and their role as a driving force for change.

Communication networks are the nervous system of the country and organizations; if they do not work well, they will suffer from Parkinson's disease.

13. Attitudes and aptitudes

You can choose the attitude
you will have in the face of
anything at all.
Viktor Frankl

Attitude is a personal choice. Everyone chooses with which one they face life. Viktor Frankl explains it very well: even if you are in a concentration camp, obviously against your will, what goes through your mind, your inner freedom, and your attitude cannot be controlled by anyone. How many people have been imprisoned in inhumane conditions and have not changed their values. Those who are mentally stronger will survive. Frankl's experience in Auschwitz and Dachau and his studies demonstrate the supremacy of the mind and inner life of each one over external circumstances and the body's physical condition. Frankl observed that those selected every morning by Nazi guards to go to the gas chambers were those who had already surrendered. When someone stopped fighting inside, they did not survive, since the executioner noticed that and executed them, because they were no longer useful for them.

By analogy with the above, those companies will survive the crises, or overcome them better, which feature greater mental strength, more cohesive teams, and a more innovative, more proactive, more constructive attitude. Those with an unfair dominance, those which are believed to be inefficient due to their privileged position or an overprotective regulation cannot be maintained nor will they maintain themselves. Those with a stronger, more proactive, and more resilient culture get ahead.

Frankl describes how he asked his patients why they did not commit suicide. We may, therefore, ask: why do I go to work? Why does our team go to work? Why did I get up this morning?

We must never forget that skills and knowledge (aptitudes) can be learned or acquired, found, that is to say, you can buy them from an external supplier outside the organization, but attitude is not sold. At best, we can ask for help from consultants or coaches, but if a person does not make a decision and choose the right attitude, there is nothing you can do, it cannot be imposed.

Let us recall that Kennedy, when announcing the project of going to the moon, he used the word *choose* and did not say they were going to try it nor did he ask what people thought about pretending to be astronauts. He made a statement, showed his willingness, and notified his determination. He made a decision, and that is where we eventually got to[44].

Forget about *yes, we can*; think rather *yes, we want to*.

That life is hard is obvious, and spending hours wondering why it is like that and why it cannot be easier makes no sense,

——————————
Attitude cannot
be bought
——————————

---

[44] Apollo 11 landed on the moon on July 20, 1969. "We choose to go to the moon not because it is easy, but because it is hard."

it is wasting time. What does make sense is to take reality as is and find out how we can change or improve what we do not like. The person who wrote Genesis thousands of years ago knew it already. In that book, we are reminded that we are here to "subdue the earth."[45]

We are lacking ambition. Healthy ambition. We are not talking about the burning desire to achieve power, status, wealth, or fame[46], but about large-scale projects that require hard work and effort to develop successfully. Ambition is not to be confused with greed. Therefore, being ambitious is neither wrong nor a sin; on the contrary, it is unavoidable to set ambitious targets, as they are essential to thrive. It is not wrong to want to go to the moon. We got to the moon, because someone chose to go to the moon, while being aware that they faced a great challenge and that it could be a failure. To get there, they needed to develop new skills and knowledge, as well as tackle unknown issues.

Generally, if targets are ambitious enough, they are never reached, hence giving us an opportunity to try them again and entering the virtuous cycle of continuous improvement. If goals are reached too quickly, it is likely that they do not deserve the qualification that they are ambitious. You can draw an analogy with stress, according to the concept handled by Mario Alonso Puig in his book, *Vivir*

---

[45] Genesis 1, 28.

[46] http://lema.rae.es/drae/?val=ambición. The dictionary of the Spanish Royal Academy provides only the first definition, whereas the Collins English dictionary considers both.

es una necesidad urgente (Living is an urgent need): there is positive stress (eustress) and negative stress (distress), and you cannot survive without the former. Thus, there is also positive and negative ambition; without ambition, without a desire to prosper, without innovation, our businesses will not survive. Just like you have to avoid negative stress and enhance the positive one, we must encourage healthy ambition and reward those who apply it, be it an innovator, an entrepreneur, or a businessman. It is sad that employers[47] in Spanish society have such a bad reputation, and, while some deserve it, an overwhelming majority of them give everything, including their money, for the business, against all odds, especially small and medium businesses.

Creating the right aptitude in an organization is certainly a task for those who lead it, but without forgetting that we all have the ability to influence someone. To be influential we must communicate our proposals, our ideas, and our views: the more reasoned and logical they are, the stronger they will be. Truth is a very powerful force[48]. You are not influential by remaining silent. Companies should establish appropriate communication channels for any member of the organization to be able to pass on their knowledge and proposals to the others. We

---

[47] Calling senior executives entrepreneurs is a misuse of the term and may even constitute a lack of respect for actual entrepreneurs. An entrepreneur is somebody who risks his or her money, not the one who administers that of others; it is not that these professionals have not earned their standing, but they should not be confused.

[48] That truth imposes itself on evil is a recurring idea in the thoughts of Karol Wojtyla (John Paul II).

must have both vertical and horizontal communication channels. Within this framework, one can define a leader as the person who leads others to choose the right attitude.

Everything can happen to us in life, and many things are beyond our control. The only clear thing is that we will always have an inner strength based on our values to address what is happening to us. Whatever happens, the only thing you really have is what is on each one's mind, will power, and knowledge. To keep that takes practice and mental gymnastics, because if you do not, it is lost, as it happens with physical shape.

> Leader is who inspire others to choose the right attitude

The most dangerous thing against a positive attitude is our own inner conversation. If we say to ourselves that we cannot, we will not. If in our team or in our organization you breathe and feel a negativity vibe, it is hard to move forward, let alone develop an innovation. However, it should be clear that transmitting values has nothing to do with selling the milkmaid's tale or deceiving staff with false promises.

14. Hope

Why did you get up
this morning?

This morning we could have chosen to stay in bed, but we didn't. Why? Because we did not have a choice or because we are excited about something and want to change the world?

Every morning, when we get up, we can choose between two options and only two: Today can be a great day or this is a disaster and this world is meaningless. Every day we can choose if we want to improve, contribute, build, learn, and help, or else destroy, vegetate, pullulate, complain, destroy ourselves and others.

Yes, this is how it goes, and this decision is made consciously or unconsciously throughout daily life and by everyone, even if most of them do not know it. Each person chooses whether life is meaningful or not. Nihilists consider that it is not, and there are many today. Sartre, who was a very clever man, came to that conclusion: this is absurd. At least, he did some thinking and came to a conclusion. Now, they sure are terribly wrong: it does make sense. They often claim that the world is full of misfortunes. And that is certainly true, but each of us, individually or together, can increase, minimize, or avoid them; we can even build good things. Tragedies and misfortunes are only one part of reality; the other is a world full of light, opportunities for growth, wealth creation, challenges to take on, others to help. You can see the carpet upside down or right side up. If you turn a beautiful Persian rug, there are only knots and chaos, you can by no means imagine the beauty on the other side.

We can choose to become a builder, to actively participate in the creation, in enjoying our work and our effort, or we can choose to be destroyers and bitter. Each morning, let us choose the mystery of life, without trying to understand everything. Why does God remain silent before so much evil? As regards God's silence, not even Benedict XVI knows how to answer that[49]. Nobody knows. But we do know that you can do many positive things every day. Some are very simple, yet difficult, such as politely greeting people we meet, although some may be a little boring or even intractable. It makes sense to help others, it makes sense to make other people's life easier. It makes sense to create wealth, it makes sense to share it. It makes sense to smile. It makes no sense to see only the bad side of things.

I insist that you read the book by Viktor Frankl, *Man's Search for Meaning;* how much wisdom on a few pages! The positive influence of this man, who learned what he explains in terrible circumstances, in the Nazi death camps, is tremendous. Never get discouraged, because it all makes sense. Never give up. If you think about it, there is no other choice. Accepting the mystery of life and seeing how wonderful it is. If we are not excited about something, we will

---

[49] www.vatican.va/holy_father/benedict_xvi/speeches/2006/may/documents/hf_ben-xvi_spe_20060528_auschwitz-birkenau_sp.html

not do anything, because we will not transmit any hope to our fellows to begin with. You cannot share what you do not have.

We are rational animals, not vegetables

Being excited about something is to hope for a better future, hoping to achieve something especially appealing. The hope we are talking about here has nothing to do with being a dreamer or being enlightened. As Pope Francis says: "I am not enlightened,"[50] but you have to be a little crazy and be some kind of a maverick; as Steve Jobs said: "The people who are crazy enough to think they can change the world are the ones who do."

Humans need challenges and dreams, we need to fill our lives with meaning and all our organizations as well. We are rational, not vegetating animals. A rational animal cannot feel fulfilled when behaving like a vegetable. Let us behave like humans, use our brains, think. Laziness is always a mental thing. Not using your brain is the worst thing you can do. But we must not fall into rationalism or perfectionism either; it is also necessary to accept the mystery and our limitations. We must learn to manage imperfection, our own and those of others[51].

---

[50] Interview by Henrique Cymerman. *La Vanguardia*, 06/13/2014.

[51] In this regard, the books by Gabriel Ginebra are interesting: *Gestión de incompetentes* (Incompetent people management), Libros de Cabecera, 2010, and *El japonés que estrelló el tren para ganar tiempo* (The Japanese who crashed the train to gain time), Conecta, 2012, Best Business Book Award.

Some sow and others reap[52]. We often do not see the fruit of our work, but there it is, because if nobody sows, nobody eats. Everyone's contribution is important, even if we do not see it and even though the person making it does not personally collect its fruits. But, if you do not sow, neither yourself nor anyone will pick any fruit. Do not focus on the most immediate things, but look at them on a medium and long term. Life on our planet will not end with us.

What we do at every moment is important, because everything adds or subtracts; it is never irrelevant, there is no zero sum. Therefore, you have to look for the logic and meaning of our actions. Let us ask ourselves once in a while: "Why am I doing this? What is the point?" Because everything has to make sense, everything transcends; sometimes we do not see it or do not understand it, but if we think about it, we will see that it is so. Yes, our actions, our projects must have a purpose, an aim, a reason, and this must be positive. If we partake of God's creative power by contributing something, we will feel better and build a more efficient organization, a more human city, a more prosperous region and country, ultimately, a better world.

Many US companies have a mission and explain this unapologetically. For example, our mission is to improve the world by providing the best communication systems. The first time a colleague from an American consultancy told me that his company's mission is to promote the use and explain the benefits

---

[52] John 36-38.

of unified communications I thought he was enlightened and exaggerated, but then I thought that this man was clear about his goal and about what he did.

I was very impressed by the paper of my colleague, Tim Lewis, in Chicago in 2007. Lewis, an African-American from Alabama with a great physical presence, entered the conference room and crossed it from the back with a red rose in his hand. When he got up the platform, everyone was impacted, while waiting for what he was going to tell us. Then, he reached into the pocket of his jacket, pulled out an envelope with rose seeds, and let us choose between the rose and the seeds, between a beautiful flower, which would fade within a few days and would end up in the trash bin, or seeds to plant in our garden, which we would have to water, wait for the rose bush to grow, and prune it, but which would give us a few flowers each year. Choosing the rose means to opt for an immediate but fleeting benefit, without effort, a mistake. Hope for the long-term—with regard to the seeds envelope—and tenacity are the right choice.

When we are tired or discouraged, we should rest, get some fresh air, and start again.

15. Proactivity and influence

Being proactive is to clear
the table after eating
without mom having to
remind us again and again.

Being proactive is to clear the table after eating without mom having to remind us of it. You have to take the dish, throw the remains away, rinse it with some water, and put the dish in the dishwasher; then, repeat the action with the glass and cutlery. After that, you have to collect the jar of water, bread, and napkins. It is really simple and obvious that it must be done. Dad can also remember it; for Dad, that action means already being a little proactive. Dads are not usually those who realize the need to clear the table.

Being proactive is to realize that you have to do something and do it without anybody having to tell you nor even hint at it; especially without anyone ordering you to do so. It is certainly a great virtue that Stephen Covey has listed as the first habit of highly effective people. The opposite of being proactive is being reactive, trailing behind.

Being proactive is to have initiative. Thinking for yourself, adding, and not subtracting. Contributing, because you move back, if you do not advance. But it is no good if someone helps you go on, that is cheating; they should, at best, give us a boost.

Everybody can contribute and be influential

To be proactive you do not have to be older nor autonomous, nor rich or independent. It is simply a matter of will and, above all, practice. It is very easy to forget to be proactive, as it is very easy to lose shape.

One of the main excuses for not being proactive is to consider oneself an errand person or a poor subcontractor[53]. "I just do what I am told and, therefore, cannot decide anything." That is a great delusion for not leaving the comfort zone. You can act freely not only as regards many small aspects of everyday life, but you can have a proactive attitude and be influential even in large organizations. That is to say, one can proactively suggest a lot of improvements or actions. You just have to start by proposing an action or an amendment. To propose something is to notify others of a positive idea; it is as simple as saying: "I have noticed this, I have gone over the issue, and I think we could obtain an improvement or benefit, if we act in a certain way or modify this procedure or this habit."

Everyone can contribute. Specifically, those people who are performing a task are the ones who know it best and should comment most on the matter. We must encourage those people to tell us the difficulties they face and to discuss how they would solve them.

---

[53] Poor is not the word I wrote the first time.

A good leader should promote proactivity in his team. It is very easy to do; just ask and take into account the views and proposals of the team. The best way to ask is when doing on-site visits at the different workplaces. You have to walk through the organization, offices, and factories, and keep in touch with the team. You cannot ask for proactivity and collaboration if you are locked in an office, isolated. You have to open the communication channel and, to that end, be in contact with your people. For collaboration to occur, you must first have established communication, but there is no communication without previous contact: to contact, communicate, and collaborate.

> A good leader should promote proactivity in his team, asking their opinion

We have to reward proactivity, recognize it, and foster it. Everyone can contribute something, can be influential; they simply have to speak; it seems easy, but it is not. As John F. Kennedy said: "One person can make a difference, and everyone should try." My children read that sentence every time they open the refrigerator door, something they constantly do, where we have a magnet that we acquired when we visited the Presidential Library in Boston[54].

> Contact, communicate, collaborate

---

[54] www.jfklibrary.org

16. Making decisions

In English, you can take
or rather make a decision.

For me, it is an unfathomable mystery how decisions are made; to be more precise: I am referring to my astonishment at the lack of logic with which many decisions are made.

In English you say *to make a decision,* whereas in Spanish we speak of "taking a decision." To me, it is not the same. The basic meaning of the word *to take* is to catch or grab something by hand, but another of its meanings, according to the dictionary of the Royal Spanish Language Academy is "to choose some of the things that are offered at will."[55] At will means "a will which is not governed by reason, but by appetite or whim."[56] Thus, unfortunately, we take decisions, that is to say, we choose while being too influenced by passions, emotions, desires, whims, ideologies, instead of building decisions, assembling (*armar*) them, as they would say in South America.

---

[55] lema.rae.es/drae/?val=Tomar. Ordinary mortals do not know that, according to the RAE, this verb has 39 different meanings, hence being highly polysemous in Spanish. The copy editor insists that, combined with decisions, it perfectly expresses the idea of thinking and deciding. But an analysis of reality confirms that today's decisions are not sufficiently pondered and poorly thought out.

[56] lema.rae.es/drae/?val=arbitrio

In fact, I think we should never just take decisions. We must always make (build) decisions. [57]

Making a decision is a process, a job, which should include the following stages:

1. Defining the reason, why we must make a decision. We have to look for the causes that justify the need to make a decision. Defining the problem to be solved: where we are and where we should head to.

2. Matching all options we are encountering. Advantages, disadvantages, and consequences of each, including the option of doing nothing, which is almost never the right thing, but it should always be considered, because the consequences of inaction are deducted by analyzing it. It is useful to prepare a table comparing the different alternatives.

3. Choosing the best option.

4. Implementing the decision.

5. Monitoring the results. Adjusting the decision based on the results obtained.

I emphasize that decisions should be prepared thoroughly by applying logic, analysis, and common

---

[57] Resorting to a literal translation or a word-by-word comparison between languages is not correct from an academic point of view, but I allow myself this license, as I believe it is a graphic and compelling way of explaining the importance of this matter. How many times did I make the mistake of saying *take a decision*, when translating in a hurry, rather than *make a decision*. I hope I get it right from now on. Lest anyone be misled, my grades in language and literature were always rather on the low side.

sense. Knowingly, which comprises intuitive knowledge[58]. Intuition is not the same as precipitation.

Some of the difficulties we face to change or improve decision-making are:

- The ideological element.
- Fads and cue-taking, that is, the tendency to do what everyone does.
- Proposals that are too revolutionary.
- The desire to satisfy everyone.
- A servant's mentality.

How many decisions are taken in advance depending on the ideology of those who need to make them. First, you decide and, then, you seek arguments to defend the position. I recommend the books by José Antonio Marina, because they first investigate and then draw conclusions. A shocking example is the necessary labor law reform in Spain. Unable to define a flexible labor market, which, in keeping with the times, ensures adequate protection of workers without destroying companies, a legislation which is inefficient and generates unemployment is left unchanged and is not replaced by one that favors job creation. The fact is that the ideological foundations are kept anchored in the problems and challenges generated by the industrial revolution of the 19th century. The situation is scandalous: you are not even allowed to have provisions in your accounts for possible compensations. A minister, whose name I do not want to mention, even hinted that they should

---

[58] For further information on this matter, you can read the book by Malcolm Gladwell, *Blink. The Power of Thinking without Thinking*, Back Bay Books; 1st edition (April 3, 2007).

not be considered deductible expenses. This situation destroys small businesses and self-employed people with employees, whereas large oligopolies fare great this way.

Let us never stop analyzing the reality and problems we are facing and let us draw our own conclusions, based on the right advice. How many people defend an absurd position, because it is what their party, their alleged ideology, their company, their boss, or their religion is defending, without even considering the question whose answer is sought. Sometimes, it happens that a position is not proven, it is assumed that the boss or headquarters want "that." Decisions are made based on assumptions.

Another emotional factor is the fear of being different and not doing what everyone else does. In information technology, this phenomenon is particularly note-worthy. For example, big brand names have a greater market share in Spain than in their home countries. It is easier to justify one's commitment to a well-known brand than to another which is less famous, even if its solutions are clearly better. People are afraid of being different, even if the distinction is caused by the pursuit of excellence.

We have to be very careful with revolutions, as they always include an element of chaos and disorder;

Evolution versus revolution

---

thus, it is advisable to avoid and anticipate them. Immobility leads to revolution. Reality teaches us that excessively abrupt changes are not good at all, because things have to keep running: innovating or improving does not mean to break everything. It is always better if something works fairly well or somehow than if it does not work at all. It is never good to cause chaos. What we need to do is evolve. Breaking everything is a temptation we must overcome. We must reject doomsday or categorical approaches that are based on beliefs that nothing works or that everything must be changed.

Decisions have to be right above anything else. We cannot succumb to the temptation of trying to satisfy all parties concerned. Consensus is not always possible and, when it is not, we should explain and *sell* very well certain decisions. When you have to change things, there will always be those who feel aggrieved, rightly or wrongly.

In Europe, we have lived under feudal regimes for centuries and, later on, under ferocious dictatorships for some more or less prolonged periods. The worst legacy of these sociopolitical systems is serfdom, which translates into an attitude that still persists. It is the legacy of a past to be overcome. You cannot go on worshiping excessively political power or dominating companies, many of which have not gained their dominance, since they come from former monopolies. There is an unaltered tendency to consider appropriate everything that comes from economic power (dominant market position) or political power and, thus, to render blind obedience, as was done with regard to the feudal lord.

I suggest that we change our approach, that we stop taking decisions and move on to making, building, or assembling decisions. Decision-making is a process, and a methodology should be applied. It is essential to perform a cold and dispassionate analysis of the problems we encounter and note down the challenge and alternatives, including that of doing nothing, as well as the solution in writing.

Finally, do not forget that decisions are not eternal. We must adapt them to the changing environment and adjust them as needed for them to remain valid.

17. The stool

No one can serve two masters.
Matthew 6, 24

A traditional stool has at least three legs, it does not stand with just two. It is necessary that a supporting area is created and, for that, three support points are needed at least.

Our political system—according to Western democracies—is a system with three powers; legislative, executive, and judicial. We believe in the separation of powers: some determine the rules of the game (legislative power), others apply them (executive power), and a third branch dictates whether or not they have been applied correctly (judicial power). The more independent the three are among them and the less obscure relationships there are between them, the better the system works. According to Winston Churchill, this is the least bad political system that has been developed to date.

A building is also built by three players: the owner-developer, the architect, and the constructor. Traditionally, the owner-developer hires, on the one hand, an architect and, on the other, a constructor (contractor). The architect, by providing their expertise, embodies the requirements and needs of their customer in a project and then checks that the works are carried out within the given deadline and in accordance with the drafted project, hence assuming the site management.

The constructor erects the building. There should not be any type of relationship between the architect and the constructor, except for the common interest in offering the customer (owner-developer) a good service and in correctly executing the project without any budget deviations and schedule delays. Similarly, when performing any other type of project, there should be three actors, each with a well-defined role: the developer-owner, the team of independent experts (engineers and consultants), and the installer-systems integrator.

The economic flow between the three parties is very important, as is shown in Figure 2. The owner-developer pays, on the one hand, for fees charged by independent professionals (architects, engineers,

Figure 2. Project management model that ensures their quality control.

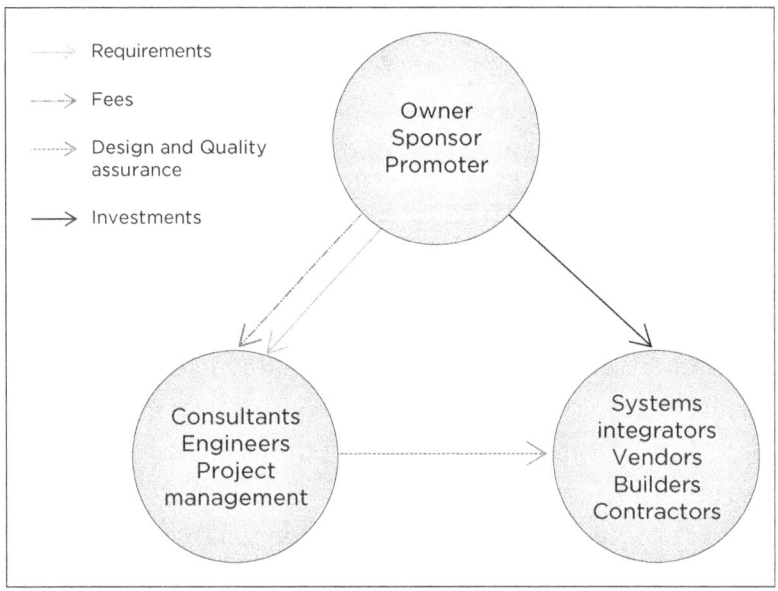

and consultants) and, on the other, for contractors (constructors, installers, integrators). There should not be any economic flow between the latter two to avoid conflicts of interest. Professionals should never be on the payroll of contractors, and for many years it has been like that.

With the so-called "turnkey projects," this good practice is lost; in this type of project, the contractor is also responsible for providing the project management team; thus, the natural power balance is broken and one of the legs disappears, as shown in Figure 3. Everyone tends to serve the paymaster; if the architect is paid by the constructor, they will show the tendency or temptation to defend the constructor's interests, be they legitimate or not, before those of the owner-

Figure 3. Malpractice scheme in project implementation. The result quality is not guaranteed.

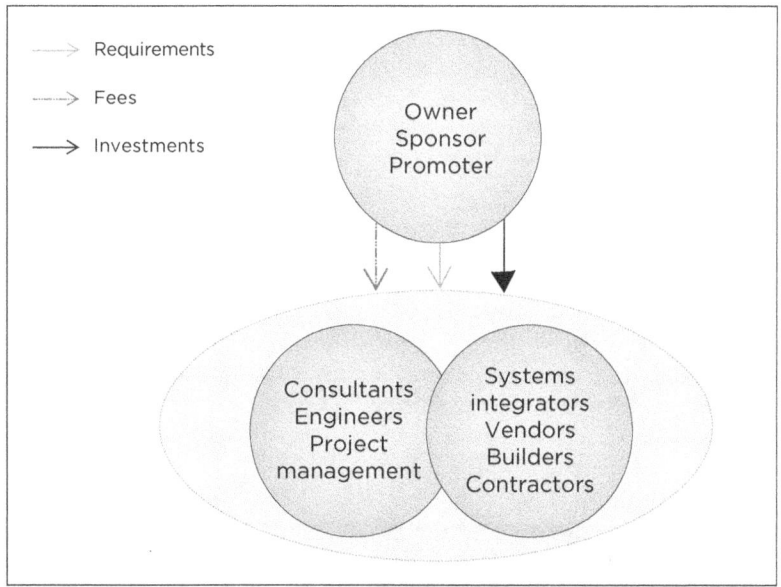

developer. I am aware that this practice has spread not only among private companies, but, what is worse, in public administration.

Another practice, which is not so manifestly incorrect, although uncomfortable and awkward, is that the contractor assumes the engineering and consulting costs, but not the service itself. In those cases, a clause is incorporated into the specifications, which states that the owner will freely choose the advisors they deem appropriate, but that the contractor shall assume and pay the consultancy fees; to avoid misunderstandings, these must be established in writing. The owner is not saving money with this practice, rather the opposite happens, since the contractor must reserve a margin to offset administration costs, but if they manage it that the consultancy item does not appear on their accounts, there must be some reason for doing that.

In short, you need three points to build a solid structure. Do not be tempted to simplify. We have to act in a somewhat clever way, with a counter-power, with counterweights, lest there are imbalances.

18. External support

If we do not know something,
it is best to ask.

In life, we often use an external advisor, whom we call for serious issues. They are priests, doctors, or lawyers, among others. The main reason why we seek them is because we do not master the subject for which we need help or we think it is beyond us.

External support provides a great advantage: dispassion. It is very important to consult people who are not directly involved in affairs, since emotions and passions are very bad counselors.

For example, to resolve conflicts it is very useful to have the figure of a mediator, since it never occurs that one of the two parties is absolutely right and it is always possible to find a third way before hurting everyone.

Another reality which is solved by hiring external consultancy services is the lack of experts in all subjects within the organization. From an economic point of view, it would be impractical and, on the other hand, they would not really be experts, since true experience is gained by addressing similar projects, but in different environments. To be a true expert you must have seen the world. In this sense, in most large organizations there is a need to open the windows and let the air circulate with new ideas. In rooms that have been closed for a long time, the air we breathe is unhealthy. To keep people trained and prepared, who are acting only occasionally, is very complicated. A fire chief told me once that the hardest part of team management was not to extinguish a fire or act in case of an emergency, but to keep the firemen quartered; the challenge is how to keep them active and avoid conflicts between them for hours on routine tasks or training.

Some people look for a consultant who tells them how handsome they are and to draft a very beautiful and spectacular PowerPoint presentation with what they want to hear. That is, what they are actually looking for is a flatterer or a communication expert. They are not interested in a person who analyzes, helps them to reason and find solutions, and enjoys academic freedom. A true consultant, a trusted advisor says what they truly believe, in a well-argued fashion and according to the best of their knowledge, free from conflicts of interest. The independence of external advisors is key; you cannot serve two masters.

Independent quality advice has an undeserved reputation of being very expensive; if you only look at the price per hour, it may even seem exaggerated. It is the story of the factory manager whose machine has stopped working, which has stopped all production. The good man, frightened as he was, began to call one mechanic after another, and they all searched the fault for hours. After several days without finding the solution, they recommended him to call a mechanical consultant, an introvert and somewhat weird person. The desperate manager asked to fetch for him. The mechanic showed up at the factory with a hammer in his hand, carefully looked at the machine, and hit it with the hammer at a given point, and, instantly, the machine was running again. The director, excited and happy as he was, asked him what he owed him. €10,000[59], said the mechanical consultant. Very uncomfortable, the director stated: "But you have only

> Honesty is a very expensive gift. Do not expect it from cheap people
> *Warren Buffett*

tapped the machine with a hammer." And the mechanical consultant explained his bill: €1 for the blow and €9,999 for knowing where to tap in less than a minute. The famous billionaire investor, Warren Buffett, would certainly agree with the moral of the story, since he says: *Honesty is a very expensive gift. Do not expect it from cheap people*[60]. It is pure logic; integrity requires knowledge and getting it requires much effort and time, so that the worker is worthy of their income[61]. Charity and volunteering need to be pursued with the needy, not with the companies[62]. Good advice has to be paid.

The support professionals or companies you hire must abide by a code of ethics, such as that of the

---

[59] 1 euro € = 1,13 US $ (February 6th, 2015)

[60] www.forbes.com/sites/erikaandersen/2013/12/02/23-quotes-from-warren-buffett-on-life-and-generosity/

[61] Luke 10, 7.

[62] If you want to make a donation or volunteer with a good cause, I suggest you help the Sisters of Charity, founded by Mother Teresa of Calcutta: I guarantee you that money is not wasted on bureaucracy and intermediaries. www.motherteresa.org/07_family/Volunteering/v_cal.html

Society of Communications Technology Consultants[63], according to which the members of this association are committed to only receive financial compensation or of any other type by their customers.

Expressed in an emphatic way, when one does not know something, it is best to ask who does know, while accepting that it is ok, that we do not expose ourselves if we ask. It is impossible to know everything about anything; so, when you have to make (build) an important decision, it is good to know the opinion of at least two or three sensible people outside the organization, since, besides knowledge, they will provide a more distant and less passionate vision of the matter. Consultants must have different and mutually complementary views. Do not forget that emotions and feelings cloud us; in fact, they can cloud the whole team, whole societies[64]. When there is fog and you drive with no visibility, the risk of impact increases exponentially and equally affects all drivers in that area. It is wise to ask and know how to get advice.

With regard to choosing whom to receive advice from, the choice is easy; simply follow Jesus' indication in the Gospel, when speaking of false prophets: "By their works ye shall know them."[65] We must find and choose consultants among those with a good reputation, knowledge, and experience, those who have done good deeds and have been successful

---

[63] www.sctcconsultants.org/?page=Code_of_Ethics

[64] Recall Nazi Germany and the notion of collective neurosis as set out by Frankl.

[65] Matthew 7, 15-20.

with their projects. It is better not to trust those who
have not done anything in
life, and they are quite a few.
This does not mean that
you should not trust young
people, because there are
young people who have
done what they had to and also provide fresh air.

> Wise people
> ask and know
> how to get
> right advice

A trick I use to assess potential partners is to ask them questions that I already know, on topics I master and whose correct answer I know beforehand. This tactic also allows us to analyze our partners' discourse coherence. To select good consultants, you also have to ask and get referrals, you have to request them from the network, the Internet; what we call *Googleing*.

19. The analysis and strategy department

I know very few organizations that have a strategy department wondering about the future of the company and setting the path to reach it. A team that helps to establish the medium and long-term objectives, forgets about the short term, and does not feel overwhelmed with day-to-day business.

Important but not urgent things

There must be people thinking about what is important but not urgent,[66] who are dedicated to analyzing how the environment changes, to observing the socio-political, technological, and demographic evolution, and to reflecting on how these changes will affect our lives, our society, and our business. Someone must be alert to the possibility that this gold mine may be over

---

[66] At this point, I was inspired by the time management model suggested by Stephen Covey in several of his books and developed further in *First things first,* Simon and Schuster, 1994. Covey classifies activities according to two core ideas: importance and urgency of the task. Depending on whether or not they have any of these features, he distinguishes four task groups:
- Urgent and important ones.
- Urgent and not important ones.
- Neither urgent nor important ones.
- Important but not urgent ones.

to start looking for another one[67]. A team that strolls through the physical or virtual world, attends fairs and congresses, keeps in touch with the university, and, in turn, knows the business itself. People who have time to think, to exchange ideas, but also who listen to the organization, who are seen at the different workplaces, who step on all domains, who receive confidences, and detect inefficiencies and areas for improvement. Covey considers strategy a primary task of the important but not urgent quadrant, whereas, for example, the opposite is a waste of time and would be located in the neither urgent nor important quadrant, the worst.

The analysis and strategy department need not be large. But their members must be open-minded people, able to question everything, imaginative, creative people with an overall perspective, of the Renaissance type. They must be complementary people with different viewpoints, multidisciplinary, and multicultural. They need not be personnel who are on the payroll or engaging full time.

For me, the need to often rethink what we do, why we do it, how we do it, what we can improve, and how technology evolves is obvious, but this is clearly not so for many people and many companies. A company with a good strategy department is Telefónica[68], which handles it very well in this field, although it has many areas for improvement, if not downright negative.

---

[67] Spencer Johnson, *Who Moved My Cheese?: an Amazing Way to Deal with Change in Your Work and in Your Life,* G. P. Putnam's Sons, 1998.

[68] www.telefonica.es. Currently, in Spain all services are marketed under the Movistar brand.

Getting useful information

While seeking strong arguments to endorse my statement about the strategy department, I inevitably stumbled across military classics, one of the areas in which the implementation of strategies is very old. The word itself comes from the Greek words, *stratos* ("army") and *agein* ("to lead, guide"), that is, leading an army. Although this book promotes a win-win strategy and not a lose-lose one, which is the one of wars, there are very wise pieces of advice from military people—all-time pure wisdom—, such as those by the Chinese general Sun Tzu[69], who concludes that "it is best to win without fighting, and that is what distinguishes a wise man from an ignorant one," and that "nothing is more difficult than an armed struggle," and more expensive.

Sun Tzu emphasizes the vital importance of information, but we are not going to discuss the methods he recommends nor advocate them. He clearly warns that it cannot be obtained from ghosts or spirits and also recommends the advantages of asking for advice: "Assess the advantages in taking advice, then structure your forces accordingly to supplement extraordinary tactics."

The most famous piece of advice of another great strategist, Warren Buffet, is "do not invest in

---

[69] Sun Tzu is the author of the famous book, *The Art of War,* an all-time bestseller of the commuter flight between Madrid and Barcelona or on the Spanish AVE high-speed train (version of the expert in Buddhisms and Eastern philosophies, Thomas Cleary, a Harvard Doctor of Civilizations and East-Asian Languages and a professor at Kyoto University).

what you do not understand," the same who states that "honesty is a very expensive gift, do not expect it from cheap people." A good strategy department costs money, otherwise it will not manage to be good. Buffett and Sun Tzu would hit it off. But the fact that this department should be well paid does not mean that it should be made up of theorists isolated in an office. In fact, its members would have to be experienced Renaissance-type scholars capable of stepping on the ground and of listening. Lest something similar occur to what happened to me two days before the opening of the Picornell pools, home to the swimming and water polo competitions during the Barcelona Olympic Games, when a senior electrician blurted out with good sense: "Four hundred days coordinating, four hundred days planning, and now I have to install four hundred sockets in two days."

Historically, the challenge was to get information, because information is power. Sun Tzu was an avowed fan of espionage. Today, there is no need to spy; it is actually a crime. Many online contents are available, if we know how to find and properly process them. The challenge is to separate the wheat from the chaff and to turn data into relevant information. There is plenty of data, too much, it is overwhelming, but the data itself is not information, as it must be treated to obtain useful information that allows you to "build" decisions.

As Ramón Archanco, author of the blog *Papeles de inteligencia*[70], explains, the current challenge is to turn

---

[70] Intelligent papers. www.papelesdeinteligencia.com

the data overload into useful knowledge, valuable information. Follow the appropriate sources and, then, select the relevant information, a task which is an art in itself.

These activities are known as "technology watch" and "competitive intelligence." The tasks encompassing that concept provide information to the strategy department, which should analyze it, draw conclusions, and "assemble" decisions. These tasks of data collection, debugging, and cooking can be entrusted to specialized companies. Although computer tools are available, decisions should not be made by a program, but you need to apply human intelligence, intuition, and vision of the move. In the United States, people would say that you need to have visionaries in the strategy department. There, being called a visionary is a praise, whereas in Spain it sounds bad, it sounds like you are an enlightened person. A visionary is someone who is able to build a mental picture of how the future will be, to deduce what changes are occurring or will occur soon. A visionary is not a soothsayer, but somebody who is able to read the signs of change, to interpret the signs of the times.

Evolving strategy

I found Colonel John Boyd's definition of strategy superb and more contemporary than Sun Tzu's[71]: "A

---

[71] John Richard Boyd, a US Air Force Colonel and Pentagon consultant during the late 20th century; en.wikipedia.org/wiki/John_Boyd_(military_strategist).

> The challenge
> is to turn the
> data into useful
> knowledge

mental tapestry of changing intentions for harmonizing and focusing our efforts as a basis for realizing some aim or purpose in an unfolding and often unforeseen world of many bewildering events and many contending interests." Boyd's thoughts, his theoretical and philosophical structure, is only found on PowerPoint slides and is based on three great principles which were developed by physicists and mathematicians:

- Gödel's incompleteness theorems[72], which in essence say that any logical reality model is incomplete and possibly inconsistent and should always be refined and adapted based on new observations.

- Heisenberg's uncertainty principle[73], which reminds us that our ability to accurately observe reality is limited.

- The second law of thermodynamics[74], which in a very abridged and non-academic manner indicates that everything tends towards maximum entropy, which is something like a measure of disorder or molecular chaos.

Of the three principles used by Boyd, the only one they explained to me at high school was that of

[72] Kurt Gödel, an Austrian-American logician, mathematician, and philosopher (1906-1978); es.wikipedia.org/wiki/Kurt_Godel

[73] Werner Karl Heisenberg, a German physicist and Nobel laureate (1901-1976); es.wikipedia.org/wiki/Werner_Heisenberg

[74] es.wikipedia.org/wiki/Segundo_principio_de_la_termodinamica

entropy, and I admit I did not understand it at the time, it sounded terrible to me that everything tends toward maximum disorder. I even challenged my biology teacher, Josep Lluís Pérez, who incidentally was a genius; he is not only one of the teachers I remember most

> If you do not move, everything degenerates
>
> *Josep Lluís Pérez*

fondly, but one who also boasts a life journey worthy of admiration[75]. Eventually, I did learn that we must make an effort to maintain some order.

Although the vast majority of us will never understand anything by Gödel, Heisenberg, or about thermodynamics—and we may possibly not even need it at all—, we can understand, however, that a strategy must take into account reality, see the world as it is, and we can interpret the principles as follows:

1. We must constantly improve and adjust our models, procedures, and forms of understanding reality.
2. We do not grasp the whole reality, we have limited access to information.
3. You need to be alert, because everything tends to maximum disorder.

Boyd's wise definition of strategy holds important concepts that should not be overlooked:

---

[75] "Josep Lluís Pérez, 77 years old: "Si no te mueves, todo degenera" (If you do not move, everything degenerates), *La Vanguardia*, 01/13/2014. http://www.lavanguardia.com/vida/20140113/54398047711/josep-lluis-perez-77-anos-mueves-degenera.html

- Strategy is something that is alive, you have to work on it and refine it every day. It must be changing.
- We must harmonize and focus our efforts to achieve a goal.
- The world is full of unexpected events and contingencies, which is disconcerting. It is impossible to have everything under control. Absolute security does not exist.
- There are competing interests. In this world, there are conflicts and competition, and sometimes highly unfair competition.

Boyd also defines the purpose of strategy: "To improve our ability to shape and adapt to unfolding circumstances, so that we (as individuals or as groups or as a culture or as a nation-state) can survive on our own terms." In other words, we need a strategy to survive and adapt better. The goal is not to work harder, but to work smarter, more efficient.

The result of Boyd's work is known as "OODA loop," which stands for observe, orient, decide, and act; thus, we are speaking of a servo system, aimed at *making* decisions and acting and, after analyzing the results, trying it again. This is an approach which is highly aligned with what this book suggests. The OODA loop will be discussed in the chapter on servo systems in the wrap-up section.

The opportunity window

Strategists have to find opportunities. They have to be a little *Fabian*. Quintus Fabius Maximus Verrucosus was a Roman general and politician who faced Hannibal in the Second Punic War (Rome against Carthage). General Fabius characterized himself as somebody who knew when to find the right moment to attack; he did not rush, he was a patient man, who waited for the circumstances to be favorable; he waited for an opportunity to arise. It is the same strategy as a hunter's, who waits for hours in their position until the catch passes by. If they rush when they see it, they are going to scare it and, if they delay their move, it will escape. Thus, they should shoot at the right time, when the window of opportunity opens and before it closes again. Fabius was misunderstood, as the people and the Roman Senate accused him of passivity, but in the end history proved him right. Being a procrastinator or being patient and timely is not the same. Not rushing into failure, waiting for a better opportunity. General Fabius did it better than Colonel Mastalerz.

There is a current of socialism that must be borne in mind and that called itself "Fabianism." Frank Podmore (1856-1910), a founding member of the Fabian Society, muses: "For the right moment you must wait, as Fabius did most patiently, when warring against Hannibal, though many censured his delays; but when the time comes you must strike hard, as Fabius did."

I hope these brief reflections, perhaps a bit complex, convince us, so as to devote the time and resources necessary to define our personal and business strategy. So that we focus on what is important but not urgent, as explained by Stephen R. Covey, when developing the third habit of highly effective people ("first things first"), and know how to find the right time, while avoiding both rush and procrastination. Without forgetting that our strategy must be flexible, an evolving strategy. It is a mistake to set a strategy and never change it, being obstinate. If you hike on a bike and do not change gear, you are not able to climb the slopes.

20. Selling Innovation

Selling is not a sin,
neither is selling dreams.

Sellers have a bad press. The are often, unfairly, considered tricksters or fraudsters, individuals that put things in front of us that are useless or more expensive than they should be. Much to the contrary, selling is not a sin, but a very worthy and also necessary activity. If a company does not sell its products, however good they are and however great their cost/performance ratio is, the company goes bust. If you do not know how to sell yourself, you do not get a good job.

It seems that there was a time, when the least prepared people were devoted to sales, as people did not stop buying. This is no longer so. Selling is very difficult; moreover, there are services, products, or ideas that are particularly difficult to sell. Change and innovation are certainly some of them, because they implicitly mean effort, risk, work, as it means to rebel against the status quo and push to leave the comfort zone, to get off the couch. You have to be very clever, "wise as serpents,"[76] if you want to complete a project that represents change. We will encounter all kinds of enemies everywhere, many people interested in the matter derailing.

---

[76] Matthew 10, 16. Jesus' advice to the apostles, when he sent them to preach change.

Sale is paramount and must be done at all levels of the organization. To begin with, you have to sell the project to the company management, as it will not succeed without their support. A sponsor is needed. For example, part of the success of Christopher Columbus was based on the fact that he knew how to find the right sponsor, which was not easy. Before Queen Isabella of Castilla bought his project, there were others who rejected it. To achieve this you have to know very well how to explain the goal of the project, its scope, the benefits it will bring, and the risks of not doing so. A suitable sponsor provides the authority and support needed to overcome the reluctance of opponents, who certainly exist.

Many management committees will only understand the concepts of return on investment (ROI), capital expenditures (CAPEX), and operating expenses (OPEX). Consequently, these aspects should always be treated, and you have to be very clear and transparent about them; you have to work on them thoroughly. If a quote approval is requested, it is very important not to deviate upwards; albeit a very common practice, it is a disgrace for those leading the project. Unforeseen events happen and must be taken into account.

The costs of a company are shaped like an iceberg, a small part of them is visible, but most of them are not. Americans distinguish between soft dollars and hard dollars, money you

---

The costs of organizational inefficiencies are very difficult to quantify and are highly sensitive issues

---

can touch and money you cannot touch, indirect expenditure and savings, as well as direct expenditure and savings. For example, you can easily see the amount of your cellular phone bill, but the hours dedicated to making calls or surfing the Internet on matters outside the scope of the company are not so easily visible, even though the cost of the hours devoted to those activities is much higher than the call or navigation itself[77]. The costs of organizational inefficiencies are very difficult to quantify and are highly sensitive issues.

Direct costs are understood and accepted without difficulty, but are much smaller (protruding part of the iceberg); indirect costs are more difficult to justify and accept, hence to sell. There is more at stake, procedural and organizational changes represent power and budget adjustments, but this is where the real money is (submerged part of the iceberg). Those projects in which you cannot submit a very low hard return on investment, of a few months or years, or those contemplating fuzzy soft factors are much harder to sell. In fact, the more innovation a project includes, the more difficult it is to sell. Following with the example of telecommunications, selling a cost audit is relatively easy, but selling a client-interaction center, which is integrated in the website and would involve adjustments to the commercial network, is

---

[77] As long as you do not navigate in exotic countries using roaming and without an adequate data bonus. We have seen bills of up to €35,000, and each September it is usual to have bills between €3,000 and €6,000 regarding only one company line.

**Check the
additions is key**

---

very difficult. Rather than a sponsor, what you need for the latter is a leader.

Oddly enough, there still are people who submit reports and offers with errors in their additions. Spreadsheets are very dangerous and should be reviewed and checked. The first thing a manager who does not like a project will do is look for errors in the amounts or inconsistencies in figures, show the report drafter up, and question its content. It is a rookie mistake that even veterans make.

Having a sponsor, upselling the product is essential, but not sufficient. It is very appropriate and smart to also downsell and sidesell the project. The fewer enemies, the better, that is to say, the more people are convinced of the necessity of carrying out the project, the less difficulties there are. Even if you have full power, imposing something is always unwise; it is easier and faster than convincing, but ultimately it entails more risks and worse results are obtained. If users are consulted, those directly affected, they will feel like they are part of it, they will feel recognized and collaborate. People like to be informed of what is happening in their organization, even if it affects them only collaterally. It is much better to convince than to impose. Imposing is the last resort, and the fewer people are affected, the better. But, if there is no other choice, you cannot give up using the staff[78].

---

[78] The staff of bishops and abbots is the pastoral sign, the stick with which to hit sheep softly and correct them so they do not go astray. It is used to accompany them back to the flock.

21. Negotiation

Perfection is the enemy of good.
Spanish proverb

Let us hope you have lawsuits and you win them.
Gypsy curse

Like arrows in the hand of a warrior,
so are the children of one's youth.
How blessed is the man whose quiver
is full of them! They will not be
ashamed when they speak with their
enemies in the gate.
Psalm 127

In this life, you have to negotiate everything. We negotiate continuously, even inadvertently and in all areas: personal, family, professional, social.

Win-win

An innovation, change, or improvement project must be negotiated to the last detail with all the players involved. The goal of negotiation is to reach an agreement, and there are three possible agreements:
- Win-win
- Win-lose
- Lose-lose

The most common thing is that people act within a win-lose framework. As mentioned above, other people, who are dominated by envy, persist in the lose-lose option. The intermediate position (win-lose) actually does not exist, as it evolves towards lose-lose.

Squeezing suppliers is a clear example of win-lose, which is, in fact, lose-lose. If you exert too much pressure on them, the buyer can be very happy with the good price they have got, but they have not understood that, if the provider works with losses or with tiny margins, they will end up reducing the quality of their services or products, or closing the business. In both cases, the buyer will also end up greatly impaired. They will need to replace the supplier, with everything this entails, or lose customers, as they have reduced, in turn, the quality of their products. The seemingly winning agreement will evolve into a losing agreement, in which both parties lose out.

Something similar is what happened to the Mayans, I guess. This pre-Columbian civilization, which died out mysteriously and was known for its tremendous cruelty, had the same god for war and for trade and cocoa called Ek Chuah. Sharing a god for trade and war is quite puzzling, as they are antagonistic concepts. That the god of commerce is the same as that of cocoa is ok, but to think that it also serves for war is a completely wrong approach, a basic philosophical error that led the Mayans to extinction; at least this way they encountered many difficulties to survive. I was introduced to Ek Chuah when I was visiting the magnificent Mayan ruins of Tulum[79], possibly the

---

[79] www.visitmexico.com/es/tulum-riviera-maya

most beautiful place I have visited, and I was really shocked at how ugly its representation was.

War is a situation that lays out how I am going to win and how my enemy is going to lose, but which, in fact, is a lose-lose, destroy-destroy, kill-kill situation. Trade and business should be the opposite: a win-win situation, which both parties profit from. The state also signs up for policies of Mayan influence; its administrators, like Mayan priests, think that by drowning taxpayers and businesses in taxes and charges they will survive, but if businesses close and taxpayers are starving, nobody will pay taxes, and the state will remain without income. We may discover that, in addition to Ek Chuah, they are also influenced by other malevolent and destructive deities, such as Ah Puch, another figure associated with war and human sacrifice, or Ixtab, the goddess of suicide. What a self-destructive culture! It is also significant that, in Mayan culture, there was more than one god associated with war; Ek Chuah had no exclusivity on that subject, he had to compete with Ah Puch. It is somewhat like the different state administrations competing on which of them is increasing taxes more.

The digital age, the Internet economy is a world of collaboration, cooperation, networking, bridging. Cruelty, revenge, pessimism, and catastrophism lead to self-destruction. Let us create a win-win environment and try not to keep an ancient world that, under the guise of win-lose, generates poverty. Ek Chuah is part of history; leave him alone, because the world did not end on December 21, 2012, as Mayan prophecies said.

Submissive contracts

There are also contracts in which pressure is put on the customer, supplier-submissive agreements. Those are typical contracts of large utilities: gas, water, electricity, and telecommunications. You cannot go along with regard to these companies, but you have to take the initiative and apply techniques in line with David against Goliath[80]. Thinking about how to rectify the situation; for example, no customer is important for these companies, but they can be a very important customer for the sales agent who manages the account, who may not receive any bonus or have to explain a lot, if they lose that account.

Negotiating with intractable people

As already discussed in Chapter 6 on the players, there are destructive people and vegetating ones, and you need to know how to treat them. If we want to learn, it may be very useful to have a look at the interesting perspective set out by the experts in negotiations, Ronald Shapiro, and his partner, Mark A. Jankowski,[81] in their book *Bullies, Tyrants & Impossible People: How To Beat Them Without Joining Them*. In that book, difficult people fall into three categories:

---

[80] I Samuel 17, 12-54. David beat Goliath, because he used a better technology and avoided a direct hand-to-hand clash.

[81] Shapiro and Jankowski are founders of the Shapiro Negotiations Institute, www.shapironegotiations.com.

1. **By constitution,** those carrying it in their genes.
2. **By situation,** those who, influenced by external circumstances, adopt an unseemly attitude, even unconsciously.
3. **By strategy,** those who, for some lawful or unlawful reason, are interested in the negotiation to break off or in a project not to progress.

The book explains in an entertaining way how to identify them and what strategies can be applied to make them change their attitude in order to be able to advance or reach an agreement. The most difficult and dangerous people are the intractable ones by strategy, because they decide to be so and use this in a malevolent way. The intractables by constitution are like a fighting bull: you see them coming and can thus keep them at bay. You can also use the dentist's technique with them: before starting with the procedure, the patient holds a certain body part and says: "We are not going to hurt each other, right, doctor?"

Faced with intractable people by situation, that is, circumstantial ones, we must find out what is going on, understand them, and seek together the best option. In an innovation process, it is very common to find circumstantial intractables; who does not defend themselves if they sense that they may lose their job with the process? The fear of unemployment is very strong, very human, and, therefore, quite understandable. It is not a good idea to commit harakiri or force someone to do it. If we think that we will have to work on something different or assume a new role, may seem an insurmountable difficulty, but can also be an opportunity to do new things or recover hopes that had been set aside, an aspect which you have to know how to show.

Mediation

During a negotiation or conflict, it is not good to have someone on the ropes, leaving them no dignified exit. This aspect was key to favorably resolve one of the most critical negotiations in the history of mankind, the Cuban missile crisis in October 1962, when the world was on the brink of a nuclear confrontation.

Before the people, on both sides, who sought war and destruction, the supporters of avoiding the latter managed to weave a balanced agreement, offering the Soviets a dignified exit by proposing the withdrawal of Jupiter medium-range missiles deployed by the United States in Italy and Turkey. The agreement allowed to defuse the tension and situation without any of the parties, Kennedy and Khrushchev, having to concede defeat. The mediation of Pope John XXIII, who created a bridge and a parallel communication channel between Washington and Moscow, was also very important, although this is an aspect that many historians and analysts overlook. Mediation is

---

Mediation is like resting on the cushion when playing billiards and being unable to make a direct cannon

---

like resting on the cushion when playing billiards and being unable to make a direct cannon. It is exciting to analyze this crisis and its resolution, and it is worth seeing a great movie[82] which was made about it. Without doubt, and for the good of all, it was a great success, and we need to learn a lot from it.

Building a proper staging

Another aspect I advise against when carrying out complicated negotiations is over-staging, both sides confronted at a table with too many attendees. Shows are for celebrations, not for negotiation processes. The only film strategy I recommend is that of good cop, bad cop; it seems incredible, but it still works. As you know, it consists in having, on the same side, a more intransigent position and another one which is more open to dialog.

Contracts

Unfortunately, agreements must be captured in writing. Shaking hands, as people say this was done in the past, is no longer possible, the risk of misunderstanding is too high. Thus, there is no other choice but to draft and sign a contract, which is a problem nonetheless, especially when the legal counsels of the parties enter the scene as well as the literalist readings. An

---

[82] *Thirteen Days* (2000), starring Kevin Costner and directed by Roger Donaldson.

agreement includes body and spirit. It has a material part, which is written in a document, but there is also a contract spirit, which is usually difficult to capture in writing; occasionally, it should not even be carried out, and this is where difficulties arise. Nowadays, "gentlemen's agreements" still exist, are necessary, and are even met. I note that whoever drafts the contract always starts with an advantage.

Good agreements have to last and serve to establish medium or long-term relationships. You cannot be renegotiating the rules of the game one by one. If agreements are really good, they are filed in a drawer and never leave it again. When someone asks what the contract says about some matter, it is a bad sign.

Clear and distinct ideas on negotiating

In short, a negotiation succeeds when you reach a balanced win-win agreement, and this requires:

- Working more on the topic than your adversary or opponent, who is not your enemy.
- You have to empathize, understand the other's position, walk a mile in their shoes.
- Seducing the law firms of both parties, which are always those with the most extreme positions, probably because of their professional practice.
- Prioritizing one-by-one contacts, the short distance. As a frivolous cologne ad goes, the same happens in negotiations, we take a gamble at short distances.
- Using mediators. Searching indirect communication channels.

- Being imaginative and creative.
- Drafting all documents, minutes, contracts, and agreements. He who drafts always has an advantage. Attack is the best form of defense. An active person is always better placed than a reactive one.
- The worst enemies are those on your own side.

22. Training and self-training

Reading is very cheap.

When we create an innovation, we not only have to sell it, but we also have to explain very well and thoroughly why we want to innovate in that particular case and show what one has to do to get the most out of it. An innovation is worthless, if it is not used properly or only used partially and incorrectly.

This is a typical error in projects related to information technologies. People believe that users will learn on their own and without doing anything. In fact, many suppliers *sell* that this is what is going to happen. Although something may be very easy to learn, you have to motivate people to learn and use it. That is, you need training. Training is closely linked to sales; when we train people on something new, innovative, we are also selling it.

Training needs to be adapted to students, the same curriculum may not be appropriate for everyone. Remember that you have to adapt the message to the receiver. Therefore, a good strategy to get the proposed innovation to succeed in an organization is to train trainers, locate natural leaders in all departments, and enable them not only to master new systems, but also to train their peers. The reason is simple: those natural leaders are very influential in their environment, are on the same level as their peers, and speak the same language. The advice of

167

a friend, of an equal, is always better accepted than that of a teacher or a parent.

In most projects, the blunder occurs of not contemplating a budget provision for training or of establishing a symbolic one. You have to invest in training, not only by spending money, but time is especially required. Today, it is possible to greatly reduce costs by using collaboration tools, organizing webinars, or making use of video.

Learning organization

Training is not only important in the context of a project or a change; in fact, it should be a continuum, an on-going thing. The concept that best explains this is the *learning organization*[83], which was developed by the American scientist, Peter Senge, in his book, *The Fifth Discipline: The Art & Practice of the Learning Organization*. It is interesting to mention that Senge has a background in science and arts, in aeronautical engineering and philosophy.

It is not only a very good practice to implement the habit of continuous learning in an organization, it is also surely necessary to survive. An organization that encourages all its members to regularly acquire new knowledge and share it with their peers from all levels, is much better prepared and stays alert to adapt to changes and, thus, remain competitive.

---

[83] en.wikipedia.org/wiki/Learning_organization

Overcoming training deficiencies by reading

We have to be aware that there are many things we do not know on an individual and collective level. The training we received, both human and academic, is manifestly imperfect; I dare say very limited, with very serious shortcomings. Since changing the educational system is not within our reach and returning to school does not make sense, let us focus on what we can do. The good news is that, if you want, you can permanently improve your training and skills and those of your family or your team. It is very easy and inexpensive: you can achieve that by reading interesting books and practicing the recommendations contained therein. Let us promote the reading habit.

In addition to the books mentioned in every chapter of this book, I added in the references a list of books which were not specifically named and a list of recommended authors.

Reading a book is a bargain, because it has a great cost-performance ratio. Moreover, you can read when you are on the move from one place to another, in the restroom, in your spare time. José Antonio Marina defined the "time junkman" concept, with which he refers to the use of downtime. In fact, when writing this book, I have applied this concept; I have written many chapters at times, when I was able to, and when I have felt like it or when I had a downturn in work. It would have been better if I had locked myself up to write a better book, but that proved unfeasible, because of my personal and professional obligations.

We apply the saying "perfect is the enemy of good," and that is why there is a book.

A book costs between ten and thirty euros in print, and from one to nine in electronic format. Doing a master's course in business administration is worth roughly thirty thousand euros in annual tuition plus a year of income, which would be about thirty thousand euros gross in the case of a recent graduate; therefore, a master's course during a couple of years costs not less than one hundred twenty thousand euros (€120,000), which is equivalent to four thousand books (of thirty euros) and one hundred twenty thousand ebooks (of one euro). A master's course is obviously not the same as some books; in a class with a good teacher and interaction with other students, you can learn a lot and, undeniably, more comfortably, but four thousand books contain much more knowledge, than they can explain at any business school, however sexy it may be to belong to the alumni of one of them and irrespective of how many relationships (networking) are established. Remember that you will have to write off one hundred twenty thousand euros. The cost-performance ratio is better in terms of reading habit than if we do a two-year master's course; the disadvantages are that it requires more willpower and is not so glamorous, but more efficient. Not everyone can pursue a master's degree or attend expensive seminars, but books and other publications are available to all.

Learning by doing is an excellent practice

Moreover, I believe we are exaggerating on the relevance

of academic training, which is too prolonged. It is not good to join the working life at thirty. It is much more educational, interesting, and fun if you work, deal with real problems, not with cases or PowerPoint presentations. In PowerPoint presentations, you do not stumble upon destroyers or intractable people. You always need to be learning, but from a given moment, this must be done in parallel with the development of a career or by addressing a real project. Conferences, congresses, trade fairs, sessions, or seminars of one or a few days also serve to learn a lot.

Training limitations to overcome

Below I briefly point out some of the gaps in basic training we encounter and which I consider most important.

Most people do not have a minimum philosophical base when finishing secondary education, and this happens against all logic, since ideas are highly powerful. Ideologies move the world. Studying philosophy, both Western and Eastern, teaches you how to think and reason. People think, vegetables do not. The brain is the most powerful tool we have. People think in terms of their philosophy of life and their culture. For example, to be able to do business with the East you must know how they reason in those areas, what motivates them.

The most powerful tool we have is our brain

171

We do not have a clue about psychology, as we take it for granted. A woman's psychology is not that of a man's. It is simple: they are biologically and psychologically different. Knowing psychology is a competitive advantage. We believe that we can learn it out of habit, that life teaches us, but we lack a theoretical basis.

That languages are important, especially English, goes without saying, but, as neurolinguists teach us, the fact is that each language uses a different part of the brain, so that the more languages we speak, the more mental gymnastics we do. Studying languages is an exponential factor of personal growth.

We have been educated with a rather negative, even very negative view. I hope that most tutors and teachers are unaware of what they do when instilling that vision, but it is such a shame. We educate to avoid mistakes ("be careful, not to do anything wrong"), but we do not educate to create, to build, to innovate. We are so worried about doing anything wrong that we forget to do good things or dare not to do them.

Habits

We should always be learning, one way or another; thus, let us acquire that habit. But even more important is to acquire the habit of thinking and reasoning. Everyone should develop their own wisdom, be able to draw their own conclusions. This requires analyzing reality and documenting knowledge and beliefs well. It is also necessary to enter a circle of continuous improvement, a virtuous circle, and never be satisfied with what you already know. Without feeling overwhelmed, we must acquire the habit of nonstop training. As the ad published years ago by a famous brand of sneakers went ("there is no finish line"), there is no finishing line as regards wisdom.

Perseverance

To learn and understand certain concepts takes time. As fruit needs time to mature, so does knowledge. Each person has their learning pace: some need more than others, depending on the subject concerned. To acquire new virtues and get rid of bad habits, you need even more time and effort than to acquire knowledge. They are processes that run in parallel. Generally, the wisest people are more virtuous. Virtue is very smart. However, it is not very smart to believe that we know much or that we are the best or even superior to others, because that is never true. Therefore, this is not a wise attitude.

> People think, vegetables no

I insist that the really important thing is to learn to think. That is to say, do mental gymnastics, as much knowledge becomes obsolete, but good habits and values are always helpful[84]. Legislation changes and technology evolves.

---

[84] In Chapter 21 on negotiation, Psalm 127 is transcribed, which tells us that, thanks to the "children of youth," we will not be confused in litigations. Spiritual authors consider that good habits are the children of youth.

Appreciating wisdom

We have already praised Solomon's great ability to mediate and resolve complicated issues, but it is also worth mentioning that Solomon once asked God for wisdom instead of power and wealth, and God was so pleased about Solomon's request that he was granted the gift, and, in addition, he had power and wealth[85]. Even when praying, Solomon prayed wisely. I pray to God that he may give us all wisdom, because we can observe a great lack of it. Wisdom may also be called "common sense," and its lack is a cross deficit, which is evenly distributed across all sectors, levels, and groups in our society and all our organizations.

---

[85] I Kings 3, 5-14.

23. Meeting management

If you want something not
to work, create a committee.
Napoleon Bonaparte

Meetings are difficult to manage. In addition, we are having an epidemic of meetings. A badly prepared meeting can end up in any way, so you should never leave them to chance. They are like horses to tame: you must tie them short, so they do not run wild. For a meeting to be successful you have to apply a strict methodology and establish a target; define an agenda, where you set the start and end time, as well as the contents of the meeting.

At the end, we must write immediately, while still hot, the minutes with the conclusions and send them, because, if you do not, after a few days nobody remembers what was discussed; indeed, we are providing some people with a great excuse for not wanting to remember. Never assume that that which was agreed on at a meeting will be fulfilled; we must pursue and demand it.

Excess participants

To be clear before proceeding: I do not like meetings. I believe that too many are held with excess attendees,

---

Meetings should not be improvised

---

some of them even absent-minded[86], and they are almost always poorly prepared. The more people attend a meeting, the worse it will be. Nevertheless, some companies insist on sending nearly a division of people, while being unaware of the bad image they offer. Take an actual example: a provider visiting a prospect with great business potential and, therefore, guessing that they have to show great interest; thus, they cannot think of anything better than organizing a great landing of people at the premises of the poor customer.

They do not realize that they are going to give the contrary impression to the one they desired; the customer will think they are poorly organized, lack coordination and internal communication, and have an oversized staff. If they are observant, the customer will detect signs of inefficiency and think: we are going to end up paying for the cost overruns that this supplier bears. In case of doubt, it is always better to be less at meetings.

Purpose of a meeting

We are convinced that meetings serve to make decisions, negotiate agreements, get information, or give instructions and can pretend really well that this is

---

[86] That is, with their mind elsewhere.

their rationale. But they are actually not the place for *making* decisions or negotiating anything serious, nor for getting information, nor are they the best place for giving instructions.

Meetings should have only two possible aims: to motivate or celebrate.

A meeting would have to be something like a social event, in which all participants express their agreement with that set out by the person presiding it, with all decisions and serious agreements established beforehand. Successful meetings are those that are a pure formality.

Of the different types of meetings that are held during a project, as regards its launch, monitoring, or decision-making, we are going to discuss its stated aim and the one I suggest for them to be a success.

For example, at project launching meetings the schedule will set the following reports: its scope and target, the timing, methodology, and the role of each participant, and that is fine with me, but there is no need to hold a meeting for this, as those are, indeed, aspects that should already be known in advance; for me the actual goal should be to "lay the first stone," that is to say, a social and motivational event to help the work team to know each other better and to cooperate with each other more fluently.

In follow-up meetings, the calling letter will mention that the point is to ascertain whether the objectives are being met and if there is no delay or lack of coordination, but we are going to fare very badly if we wait for a meeting to be held to get that information. The actual goal is to keep the team members motivated and cooperative, to avoid the creation of isolated silos.

At decision-making meetings, you should never neither make nor even discuss a decision, it will not be good, many negative vibrations can accumulate. Such meetings should be held only to celebrate that an agreement has been reached or a decision has been build.

I have attended meetings where decisions contrary to all logic were made, just because the *competent authority* wants or needs to assert itself by deciding the opposite of what the work team suggests. Those are meetings where the team trembles and those who contradict the rest fall from grace; almost nobody dares to propose anything.

Breaking off a meeting is very easy, you just need to behave like an intractable person; as we discussed in the section on negotiation, you must learn to manage and treat intractable people. In the table below, we can compare the stated and "official" aim, and that which should be applied, but you cannot mention.

Type of meeting	Official aim	Actual aim
Launching	Reporting project aim and scope	Motivating the team to work together
Follow-up	Verifying that the milestones are being achieved and avoiding lack of coordination	Keeping the team motivated and united
Decision-making	Making a decision	Celebrating that an agreement has been reached

One by one

The meeting leader, the person who convenes and manages it, must put a lot of work into it before celebrating it. The meetings that people attend to have discussions, confrontations, train crashes so to speak, are a disaster. It is better not to convene them. If there are difficulties in a project, they must be resolved in advance and in a small group. When there are too many people, they do not talk with total honesty and transparency. Many people feel uncomfortable, do not know how to notify bad news or failures, cannot convey the truth, if it is bitter. A meeting should not be a torture chamber for anyone, and we must prevent someone from being exposed. One thing is to dispatch and another to meet up with the team.

If a bomb explodes during a meeting, it is because we are doing something very wrong. You have to detect it early on and deactivate it. If you have to communicate bad news, you have to discuss it before with the bosses and those involved, so they are not taken by surprise. If you have to bring up an issue, you cannot just tell the problem, you must also present the solution.

Really important things are discussed with maximum discretion: while sipping coffee at the corner bar or at a working desk. Valuable information does not come up in a meeting, however hard you try. An anecdote should illustrate the above. On one occasion, I was invited to a private discussion, in which, for the attendees to feel comfortable and express their views, we were told that it would be governed under the

Chatham House Rule[87], a rule which was established in 1927 and redefined in 2002, and which allows you to use the information or opinions expressed at a meeting, provided they do not identify the person issuing them; peculiarities of British diplomacy and international business. I attest that the moderator took the matter very seriously. To me everything that was said was interesting, but in the public domain of all attendees, and I did not find anyone felt uncomfortable, and I do not think it was because that rule was applied. It was a debate about networking; it is a shame it did not revolve around negotiating a multimillion-dollar contract! Undoubtedly, the staging was superb, which is inversely proportional to the importance of a meeting. Good meetings are held in bars, and the greater their neighborhood-feel, the better.

Business meetings and lunches

One of my first bosses, before convening a project monitoring meeting, in which a representative of each and every one of the shareholders of the company "had" to be present (apparently, they did not rely on us), asked me how much time we would need to discuss outstanding issues and, depending on my answer, one or two hours, he would set the start time, so that we finished around lunchtime. At that set time, we had obviously not resolved anything and

---

[87] http://www.chathamhouse.org/about/chatham-house-rule

were, generally, in the middle of a heated debate; then he rose to an imposing height—he was almost two meters high—and suggested we should have lunch with the excuse that we had made a table reservation in the restaurant around the corner at two o'clock and that we were late. The debate's intensity decreased to the same extent that diners were filling their stomachs. When we were about to have coffee and a drink, my boss proposed an agreement, which, by way of magic, no participant objected to, the check was paid, and farewell until we met again, when we had to go through the whole liturgy once more. It was my turn to write the minutes and send them by fax; those were different times. Note: you have to drink little alcohol and eat something light during business meetings, wine and food binges must be left to our customers or suppliers, you think better with a clear head.

Excess staging

Meetings in a living room are very dangerous. I think sitting on a sofa—in some cases, lying—and working is incompatible; sofas are suitable for negotiating other arrangements or doing other activities. I remember the case of a CEO who had a huge leather suite in his office, and during the meetings he convened he organized the following staging: attendees sat down on the couch—or rather sank into it—and he sat on a chair, so that he was well above his partners and backlit, so it was impossible to see his face. The first time you were a little puzzled, but the second time you already noticed that the staging was copied from

The Great Dictator, the film by Charles Chaplin which shows how Hitler received Mussolini[88]. I do not know if he did it on purpose or not (it seemed so), but it is clear that, if you have to interpret the staging, this man was not looking for his partners to feel comfortable, but to reassert his authority, although his overacting highlighted his insecurity: things were not working as they should have.

Quick list of ideas to successfully hold meetings

Some clear ideas about meetings that will allow us to tackle them with more chances to succeed:

- We must convene the minimum required. If in doubt, do not convene them.
- If we hesitate to invite someone to a meeting, we will fare better if we do not.
- Meetings must be resolved in advance.
- If we fear a trap, we should have an answer ready for the different scenarios.
- We must convene them properly by means of an agenda.
- You have to write the minutes in real time and distribute them quickly. Those who write the minutes have more power and get more beneficial results.
- Disrupting a meeting is too easy, do not fall into the provocation trap.

---

[88] www.youtube.com/watch?v=54po0vQ-OqY

- Meetings with great staging are bad.
- You cannot assume that the agreements reached in a meeting will be fulfilled

24. Project development

Almost everything in life
can be managed as a project.

People permanently write and discuss on project development and management; great treaties are established and a multitude of courses, seminars, conferences, and master's courses are taught, and, nevertheless, people continue to commit blunders, and spectacular failures occur. In addition, budgets usually skyrocket and schedules are extended indefinitely.

A few examples of failed projects: trains are ordered and bought which cannot enter the stations, because they do not fit into them and collide with the platforms (this happened to the Société Nationale des Chemins de Fer Français [SNCF]); airports are built where no aircraft has ever landed and, in some cases, do not even have permission to do so, such as Castellón or Córdoba; highly expensive satellites that would have to provide a positioning service which is more accurate than the current GPS are put into the wrong orbit[89].

These cases are just a small sample of the many incidents of this type newspapers publish. On a small scale, and in all companies, a vast number of messy

---

[89] Global Positioning System.

situations occur daily, whose great majority are hidden as best as one can and covered with a thick veil.

I felt somewhat shy when tackling a chapter on this subject, but you observe so many malpractices that I have finally decided to incorporate four key ideas.

To conduct a successful project it is essential to apply a minimum of order and a very basic methodology. We must avoid cumbersome methodologies and excessive control. Those who prioritize methodology above all else is mediocre. It is about finding the balance between order and creativity; avoid excessive improvisation, but always maintain some space for intuition.

On the other hand, the methodology should not only be applied to engineering or architecture, but serves for almost everything, for example, to define a marketing plan or to market any product. The ideas discussed here have multiple applications, including personal and family life.

Synthetically, five stages can be set in a project:
1. Drafting a preliminary design, feasibility study, master plan.
2. Preparing the final design.
3. Selecting and recruiting suppliers.
4. Implementation or deployment.
5. Operation (on-going management).

It is important not to miss any stage or change their order. You may wonder about the fact that I have incorporated operation to a project, but it obviously does not make sense to have a project which is not going to be used, such as Castellón Airport, or without contemplating its life cycle.

Preliminary design, feasibility study, master plan

The key to success of a project lies in its early stages. If we lay the fundamentals properly, the foundation on which the building is to be constructed, the latter will be erected, but if we build on sand instead of rock, as the Gospel parable goes, the building will not hold storms[90]. It is interesting to observe how Jesus uses this parable to refer to wisdom and caution.

When starting a project, you have to basically answer two questions: what and why, that is to say, what is the problem, challenge, or change we need to address and what are the reasons for this need.

The most common reasons that generate the curiosity or need to tackle a project are twofold: that it does not work (or only in fits and starts) or that the case is very expensive. Sometimes, both circumstances coincide: something does not work and costs a lot of money. Examples of lack of functionality are that customer calls are not answered or that orders go astray. Meanwhile, an example of additional costs may be that the actual amount for an item has risen well above what was budgeted, without the turnover having increased.

The correct definition of the problem is essential, and often the first questions or

> The key to success of a project lies in its early stages

---

90 Matthew 7, 24-27.

problems that arise are not real. You have to compare all the information. Let us recall that to solve a problem we must first recognize that there is one and identify it: "Houston, we have a problem." You have to devote time and resources to analyze the baseline, to make as-built drawings, to identify its strengths and weaknesses.

Once we have clearly defined where we are, we must determine where we want to go; for that, we must also carry out a process of comparing the current situation with that which could be achieved using the technology, services, and products available to us. You must be open-minded, search and compare solutions and alternatives. To improve many situations you do not need to invent anything new or research, you hardly ever are the first to tackle a specific problem, others have already solved similar situations for sure, and we can draw inspiration from them. There is also no need to change everything, much less to break it: we are trying to do something more efficiently, not something completely different. Often small changes bring big improvements. You have to look at the details, they are very important.

As far as possible, since travel and time are very expensive, there is nothing better than to seek what is done here, there, and everywhere to solve similar problems. It is alright to attend congresses and conferences, visit international fairs, attend product presentations, or invite potential suppliers to present their solutions, and even to visit competitors, if they allow it. A solution never arises on its own, you must awaken inspiration.

It is essential to incorporate, from the earliest process stages on, the people directly involved, end users, those whose way of life and work can change; you have to listen to them, ask them, get down onto the play field, share their work, spend time with them, and identify where it hurts them. You have to look into their eyes, as good doctors did—and still do—.

However, you must not only think of the people directly involved, but it is appropriate to invite the entire organization to participate in the process, because nowadays all projects, especially innovative ones, affect the entire organization: it is not just about technology, but it is, above all, an organizational change, and that is where the challenge lies. We need to invite *business* people and those behind them, finance, human resources, purchasing, and marketing, among other areas.

At this first stage, it is also important to define the model of project development or organization, that is to say, who will design the solution, who will install or deploy it, who will operate and who will maintain it, and, eventually, who will manage it and who will make operational decisions.

Therefore, to develop a good preliminary design or feasibility study we must perform the following tasks:

- The study (analysis)[91] of the current situation.
- The needs study (analysis).
- The preliminary analysis of alternatives.
- The definition of the economic model, which should include the funding model.

---

[91] Significant consultants like Georges Mokhbat, president of Macom Group www.macomgroup.com, strongly recommend to use the word "study" with a positive sense and to avoid the word "analysis" due to its negative sense.

- The definition of a project development model, in which we must identify who designs, who builds, who operates, and who manages.
- The description of the recommended solution.

In short, we must get all the information necessary to decide whether or not to pursue a project.

One result of the preliminary design has to be to get the necessary sponsors, that is to say, the support of the company's or organization's senior management.

Let us recall a key recommendation: you have to take good care of the results' presentation and the executive summary. It must be clear, specific, concise, and not use mnemonics or overly technical concepts that are not understood by people without the appropriate technical training, since they will not dare to ask what they mean. Beware of errors in figures!

Preparation of the final design or technical specification

Once we have decided what we must do, we must determine how we are going to do it to get the new system or new procedures to work and run properly, hence obtaining the expected results. This requires drafting a final design or technical specification, which defines exactly the following:

- The criteria based on which the solution is designed.
- The functional requirements (what the system has to do).
- The technical requirements.
- Quality control and system acceptance testing.

- The organizational aspects. How it operates and how it is maintained, both in preventive and corrective terms.
- The administrative aspects.

If it is properly drafted, the document must allow you to solicit bids (thus, it is also called Request For Proposal, RFP), facilitate their subsequent assessment, and serve as a reference for the implementation and system acceptance stage. You should, therefore, clearly specify all aspects necessary to successfully implement a system or solution.

It is a mistake to delegate the preparation of a project to installers, system integrators, contractors, or other similar professionals, as, if they have set a fixed price, they will try to save money here and there, looking for an additional margin, which will clearly affect the outcome of the end solution. In my opinion, the only project that can be delegated to a contractor is the detail project, defined as the one collecting purely technical construction details: exact pipelines, wiring, etc., but in no case the choice of functional aspects.

As to the degree of detail that should be reached in projects, there are different criteria depending on the country. In those whose most common practice is that the same team that designs also manages their implementation, as happens in Spain, projects are less specific. By contrast, in countries with two professional teams, one that designs and another that heads the construction stage, projects are more comprehensive and detailed, as the team leading the realization must perfectly understand what the designers had envisioned. In my opinion, the first way of working is more successful, that is, making the management team control the entire project and even take care of support during the operation stage, if necessary.

Selecting and recruiting suppliers

To purchase well you have to compare. You always need to have several bids on the table, which are equivalent and comparable. It is, therefore, important to define what you want to buy, that is, draft a RFP/project; if it is well made, you should not specify neither specific brands nor manufacturers, but merely services. Thus, the process is open to more competitors. You need a shortlist and not much more than three of a kind, maximum five bidders. If it is not a public process (which are those involving a company owned by the Administration or within the Administration itself), you can opt to choose the bidders and invite them to participate. If we have consulted several suppliers during the project drafting, it will be easy to select a shortlist of three.

The procedure that certain international institutions follow is very successful, that is, launching a request for interest to then select a shortlist of all those applying and open a negotiated selection process.

You always have to leave enough time to prepare a good proposal. It is a bad sign when very little time is given to respond to a request for bids, as it denotes rushing and lack of foresight; it also produces a certain impression that a decision has already been adopted and may even lead you to think of some kind of corruption.

It is a good practice to keep an open communication throughout the selection process, as doubts or interesting proposals will always arise. We must encourage that improvement proposals brought up, since they allow you to assess the bidder's interest, value their creativity and know-how; but you should keep in mind that, if not expressly invited to do so, it is very rare that a bidder dares to contradict, amend, or propose something to a prospective buyer. It is a bad practice which is too common. If you are a bidder and have a bright idea or a breaking functionality, you must suggest it in a diplomatic manner; remaining silent is the worst option.

In the specific case of public processes, you must be careful that you provide the same information to all bidders. In these environments, I advise to hold an open session to address all doubts and, upon its completion, submit in writing the answers to all stakeholders.

Once the bids have been received, the top three are selected, thoroughly analyzed, and the bidder is invited to defend their proposal and resolve any doubts that have arisen.

Except for a public tender, in which the weight of the award rests on the price, nobody submits their best price to begin with. Ideally, you should move within an intermediate range—in terms of prices, it is good to be in the center—. Those who submit a very high price risk being discarded at the first hurdle. A few years ago, the same thing happened with those who submitted a very low bid (it was called "dangerously low bid"); with the crisis this good practice has almost disappeared, and then conflicts such as that of the Panama Canal and the Sacyr construction company arise, whose bid was shockingly lower than that of other bidders.

It is not only highly desirable, but necessary, to enter into a negotiation round. For this purpose, the best thing you can do is require itemized prices (this should be stated in the request for bids document). By comparing item by item, unit price by unit price, you can easily observe differences in opinions that the single parties use. Any details can be used to assess a potential supplier, especially if you are going to work with them many years. A good presence of your workforce is critical, both in terms of sales agents and specialists. Furthermore, it is essential to assess the quality of their bid, if it is clear, specific, and concise. There are terrible bids, which, unfortunately, are not discarded in the beginning due to the logo that accompanies them. Too many are playing the game that their dominance allows them those imperfections; but at some point this will cease to be like that; all empires, including corporate ones, fall and many others are no longer what they were.

A sign to know if we have reached a good price is if at the end of the negotiation rounds several financially very tight offers are available or, rather, that they present a similar cost-performance ratio.

If projects are technically very complex or very innovative, care must be taken with being the first at something other than the core business of the company. It is good to carry out a pilot test with the two finalists (sometimes just one is enough) and link the final choice to the results of that test.

After selecting the bidder, it is essential to forge the agreements in a contract. Which is not easy at all. The drafting of certain contracts, regarding works or services and technological projects, can last for months or even years. More aspects on this matter have been mentioned in the chapter on negotiation.

One trick to save time is to incorporate a proposed contract or, at least, the most critical clauses in the request for bids document. You may also ask bidders to attach their standard contract.

Keep in mind that delaying the choice and hire of a supplier in projects of a certain size, be it economical or technological, undermines the credibility of the project itself, the company, and the people who are managing it. The loss of credibility is absolute if, in the end, the project is not implemented. Asking professionals to work for free to then cancel a project is disrespectful and almost larceny. Cancellations must be due to very serious and highly justified reasons. Otherwise, the next time and with less crisis we may not find any candidates willing to work with us.

Deployment. Project management and quality control

Once the project has been contracted, check that what was hired is being carried out (everything that has been reported in the Terms of Reference) on schedule; as the popular saying goes: do not let them rip you off.

For a project to be successful, it is essential how the implementation or deployment stage is performed (tasks which are also known as "project management"), but above all quality control and acceptance testing are critical.

Quality control should not be left for when you reach the end of implementation, but it is a task that runs parallel to its development, as there are aspects that are not visible then, because they have remained hidden. Thus, for example, the building's foundations are not visible when the building is finished, so it is highly advisable for a qualified person to regularly check how the whole construction and implementation process is being developed; in the specific case of the building, for instance, by checking the density of the cement used in the foundation. If you perform a partial testing, it is easier for the whole ensemble to work harmoniously and to obtain the expected results in the end.

Two types of tests may be performed: in the laboratory or factory and during actual operation. Without underestimating the need for multiple laboratory tests, the ultimate test is a load test, such as parking a row of loaded trucks on a bridge and verifying that the structure holds the load. Load tests must be carried out not only in civil engineering, they should also be conducted in other industrial systems, especially in information technology and telecommunications systems. How often have we heard that a website collapsed on the very opening day! Everyone is amused, and the fact is even used as free advertising, but if you want and appropriate measures are taken, it can be avoided.

I remember that on one occasion, while managing a project in a Germanic country, of proven seriousness, I announced that we were going to start testing. Then, one of the technicians, of considerable physical proportions, told me in English, very upset and with a German accent, that they were never wrong, which is quite intimidating. The good man was sure wondering what the hell the little Spaniard was asking for. I told him that I was the person in charge there and that our common client had just hired me to ensure the system worked the next morning and that we should start to test it. Well, Murphy's Law was fulfilled, but the other way round for me: the connection failed. I had no intention of showing the good man up, but the whole thing failed and, obviously, he finished by checking all the connections without complaining. At the end, we all had a few beers, which, incidentally, are very good in that area, and laughed a while.

On another occasion, we were testing a highly innovative customer care center, which was the first facility in Spain featuring a software which was developed by Russian and Ukrainian engineers and mathematicians, who had settled in California while taking advantage of Perestroika and, soon after, became billionaires, when they sold it to a large multinational company, which had a hard time innovating, as all big companies do[92]. We carried out a first load test with half of the company calling from home and the other half answering the phone. It took only seconds before the system collapsed, although all laboratory and simulation tests had been successfully surpassed; we needed a few more months as well as stress tests until we got the system to work properly. A few years later, we ran a software update and, confident as we were, did not perform any load test. After a few days, the early-year campaign came[93], and the system

---

[92] Now, it went back to being an independent company; it seems that the multinational was confining it.

[93] At that center, it was during the month of January that the peak of incoming calls occurred.

could not stand the load; it collapsed, and my winter holidays came to an end all of a sudden, from the ski slopes to the company in no time. It turned out that a parameter was incorrectly set, hence limiting the maximum number of simultaneous conversations, so that the system collapsed. Lesson learned: when a major part is changed, the system must be tested again under maximum stress conditions.

It is necessary to note that migrations, moving from the old system or procedure to the new, are always complicated, you have to plan them in detail and perform them very carefully. Provisional or interim solutions are unstable and difficult to manage. Maintaining two systems with the same parallel function is an overexertion. We people from electronics know that most components are burned in transit, during the launch of an equipment. Be very careful with transitional periods and false starts.

A sentence that should never rule during the test stage is "nothing works," because it creates discomfort and nervousness; we must avoid doomsday messages. Moreover, it is always a lie; the system does not work, because there is a critical component which fails; thus, you must locate and solve it. Once it is solved, you have to go through the whole testing again, because, especially in information technology, an error masks others.

When putting a new system into operation (which is not tantamount to the end of the project) is completed, you should celebrate it. Innovative projects that represent significant changes must be

---

Never is true than "nothing is working"

---

inaugurated. People usually do not do if often. Only great things are inaugurated and, usually, with little presence of those who have contributed the most to them. Too many medals are handed out to those who have not partici-

> Inaugurate an innovative project is a must

pated, whereas those who have broken their backs on the project are missing some hugs.

The opening is a very important part of promoting, both internally and externally, an innovative project. We must take care of it and be generous with the cocktail. When something succeeds, we should celebrate and explain it. If the supplier asks to write a success story or bring potential customers for a visit, you should not say no.

And, then, rest for a few days and take on the next challenge.

Operation

When a system is operational, you not only have to keep it running properly, but, above all, we must follow-up on the results being obtained.

There are two levels of maintenance, preventive, to avoid malfunctioning, and corrective, to restore service when an incident has occurred.

Shortly after the life of a system has expired, we must address adjustments and readjustments to resolve errors or inefficiencies that are detected with daily practice. For example, in technological solutions—within the world of software applications—users often use tools differently than analysts had thought they would. Therefore, the operating model must include how the new system will be managed and who has the authority to decide on implementing changes and adjustments.

Moreover, things do not work alone. You have to monitor them so they do not degrade. It is important to make them evolve. It is always better to slowly climb a mountain on the gentlest side than facing a vertical wall. If we do not go up a little bit every day, in the end we will encounter the mythical Eiger North Face[94]; it is smarter to go up with the Jungfrau funicular railway[95] than climbing it all the way. The intended result is the same, to reach the top. That is, the smartest thing is to be trained and overcome difficulties: climb the mountain slowly and on the easiest side.

It is a big mistake to freeze an improvement or a new system, when it has been put into operation. The work teams are dismantled, instead of resizing them to the new stage, and people think that they are already finished. The importance of on-going management is underestimated. One of the typical accusations made to the consultants is that they leave after launching new organizational applications and, if problems arise, they do not know anything. It is important that both parties, consultants and customers, understand

---

[94] The Eiger wall is known as the wall of death, the killer wall, the deadliest mountain in the Swiss alps. To overcome it you not only need to be highly prepared, but, above all, pretty crazy. youtu.be/ Zxb4Oui6m6o

[95] www.jungfrau.ch

that they have to align engineering and consulting services, the third leg of the stool, with the systems' life cycle. It always adds value to be able to rely on those who have designed the systems and solutions. Thus, we must set up follow-up and monitoring teams. By the way, good consultants, consulting *boutiques,* do not leave, they establish long-term relationships with their customers.

25. Crisis management

The important thing in a nuclear crisis
is to cool off the reactor.

Crises occur in all life projects and circumstances, and we must learn to manage them. Amid the storm, the important thing is that the ship does not sink, to minimize damage, try to get out of it or at least, its most active part as soon as possible. Storms are not eternal, crises are not either, they pass, and then you have to reset, repair damage, get back on track, and move forward.

If I remember it correctly, it was on March 1, 1988 when I started to work at Ascó nuclear plant, in the province of Tarragona, on the banks of the river Ebro. At that time, I was twenty-four years old and, after a few weeks, when returning from lunch and going through the entry checks to the premises, I learned the most important thing I know about crisis management. The power plant had a double safety ring. The first is encountered when entering the premises with your vehicle. Once the car is parked, you have to enter the actual plant on foot; for that, you have to overcome a metal detector and, then, a detector of explosives; finally, you open the door with the personal magnetic card. That day, just when I was introducing my card in the reader, a tremendous noise was heard and everything trembled. I was absolutely paralyzed[96]

---

[96] To feel paralyzed during an emergency is bad.

and thought that I might have done something wrong. Behind me came the head of electrical maintenance, Lluís Olivé, who howled at me to get away and react, while informing me of what happened: a reactor trip had occurred. Apparently, there was a problem with the output transformer and it had caught fire. As the electricity generated could not proceed, there had been an automatic shutdown of the plant, the granite blocks of the reactor core had fallen to stop the fusion of uranium, and the secondary circuit valves had opened and released a large amount of vapor to the atmosphere. I would like to explain that it was non-radioactive vapor, as it corresponded to the secondary circuit that is not in direct contact with the reactor core. The show impressed me. The problem is that the matter did not end there. Although the reactor shuts off automatically, the crisis continues, because the reactor has a high temperature and, if it is not cooled down, it can melt; and if it melts, farewell to the plant (that is what happened, in part, at the US Three Mile Island plant on March 28, 1979; what happened at Chernobyl I already mentioned in chapter four).

I would like to point out that I am not an expert on nuclear plants and that I only use the anecdote to illustrate what I want to explain. What I know about this matter I learned during the two years I worked at Ascó as person in charge of telecommunications, a very enriching experience that, I recognize it, has influenced me very positively. And, if one thing has stuck in my mind, it is that, when there has been an automatic stop, you have to cool down the reactor to avoid greater evils. From that point on, we can worry about fixing the situation. Reacting and cooling down are key words when a crisis occurs. To cool anything down requires time and resources.

There are different types of crises: economic, personal, religious, and family crises, among others. It does not matter if those that one faces are more or less intense and complicated than those of others, they are our own and we have to manage and overcome them. All crises feature an internal, personal part and an external one. You can act on your own, but you often cannot on external factors. You can act on your emotions; on those of others you can only have an influence, and the best thing anyways is to cool down and calm the situation. Remember that it is important that the reactor does not melt. For example, that nobody has a heart attack. I remember that, in the disastrous opening of the renovated Olympic Stadium in Barcelona, in 1989, a fellow of the organizing committee had to be evacuated by ambulance to the hospital, because, when he saw the mess, he suffered an anxiety attack; eventually, it was just a shock and, three years later, in 1992, the Barcelona Olympics were a success that has not been beaten as yet.

We could say that people work in a rather similar way to a reactor. It may seem surprising, but with a little explanation it will become clear. A nuclear power plant is capable of producing a large amount of electrical energy, which is used to create a lot of wealth and prosperity, but, at the same time, it is very complicated and, if it breaks, because it is not properly cared for or used incorrectly, it can cause huge disasters. People are also very complex, and we also have a great capacity for wealth creation and, consequently, can also break or organize great tragedies.

Crises-generating tiredness

A stressed person or one who intends to do more things than they are able to, neglect themselves, and do not get enough rest; thus, it is more likely that they become ill, that they make a mistake, that something breaks, or that this impacts on the work of the whole team. If the plant's maintenance tasks are decreased with the idea of getting more energy, in the end things break somewhere and a reactor trip occurs or worse. People also require maintenance. Covey says that the seventh habit of a highly efficient person is *sharpening the saw,* that is, to rest.

Bad practices in crisis management

Some things should not be done when dealing with a crisis. In fact, it is easier to know what to avoid than what to do. Although several of the ideas I suggest below have already been discussed, I think it is worth insisting on them; indeed, humans learn based on repetitions.

In the magnificent film, *The Chorus,* the lousy hospice director, Rachin, advocates an action-reaction, eye-for-eye, tooth-for-tooth strategy and immediately punishes any mischief of some kid; the consequence is that he fails to educate his pupils and increasingly loses control of the situation. Heated reactions when dealing with people are never the most appropriate ones. You always have to take some time, even if it is just a few seconds, to analyze the situation and the alternatives available, with their advantages and disadvantages, to then make a decision. I emphasize Viktor Frankl's thoughts: success lies in what is done in the space of time between the impulse to act and your actual action. That is, how we react, how we analyze the situation, and which decisions we make (build) to deal with it.

Another attitude that you should not have in a crisis is to ignore the nature of the problem or not to use the appropriate technology to solve it. It is the mistake of Colonel Mastalerz, which is described in the first chapter.

Moreover, doomsday approaches or despair do not fix anything. The sentence "nothing works" is never true.

You should also avoid overacting, although in many cases the temptation to stop everything is strong. For example, if a nuclear reactor trips, a disturbance occurs in the entire electrical system of the country, and we must prevent the imbalance that has been generated from triggering other plants as well as the domino effect from producing a power outage. But to avoid the unexpected shutdown of another power plant what does not make sense is to stop it manually; thus, what you always have to do is isolate the problem, not amplify it.

I have always considered those wayward skiers who participate in the Olympics quite funny, as they represent tropical countries, where it never snows, and halfway skip a gate, but, far from throwing in the towel, slow down as best as they can, recede, that is, go up the slope and pass again where they should have before, and pass the gate in their second attempt. I think that, with their funny attitude, they teach us that sometimes it is important to participate and reach the goal, it is important to finish what has been started, that you have come this far and that nothing happens if you make a mistake; it is possible and often very good to correct oneself. That if it goes wrong, I will try again. I think this attitude is better than that of an outstanding person who loses composure when making a mistake, breaks the stick, or throws the helmet against the protective fence. In a crisis situation, it is better to act with humility than behaving like a diva.

Good practices to address the crisis

A good practice is to remember that there are other people who have faced much tougher difficulties and challenges and have overcome them. At a conference, I heard Rudolf Giuliani, mayor of New York, say that, when the attack on the Twin Towers on September 11, 2001 occurred, that night he remembered World War II and thought that only a few buildings had fallen, that the rest of the city continued as is, and that they would, most likely, recover. He also talked about how important it is to be on site to know and assess what was happening. The leader must be on the ball.

It also helps not to forget that there is a relationship between the intensity of the storm and fertility or the benefits to be gained. In the tropics, where heavy rains occur, nature is particularly fertile and generous. Using the analogy of the storm, there is, therefore, a direct relationship between how deep or complicated a crisis can be and the possibility of personal and organizational growth involved. Overcoming serious problems enriches you, unites teams, and makes us more resilient. There is a saying that goes: when a door closes, a window opens. That is, there will be a new opportunity after the crisis.

The Republic of Venice (from the 9th century to 1797), which in its heyday in the 15th century was a world power, called itself Most Serene Republic of Venice. I have not managed to find the reason for that title, but its form of government has been widely studied and was based on the counterweight of a council, the *signoria,* to avoid that all the power rests with one man, the *doge.* In any case, linking the term serenity to power seems quite appropriate to me. The government or leadership has to be serene, especially in times of crisis.

Even if it is a somewhat collateral aspect, I cannot help but provide a note on personal crises. When one goes through a personal crisis, there is a strategy that always works: helping others, because there is always someone more needy than yourself. To give without expecting anything in return always works very well. What does not work is to think that things are not going well, because everyone is against us or that it is other people who must solve the problem.

Crises warn us

Crises warn us; just watch out for the signs, which are always there, although sometimes they may be very difficult to detect. Some crises can be avoided or at least minimized, and some cannot, but if you have seen them coming, they do not catch you off guard. In his book, *La vida, un slalom* (Life, a slalom) (published shortly after his death in 2006), Francisco Fernández Ochoa[97] says that life is about overcoming difficulties, slalom gates, one challenge after the other. It is a good tactic to tackle it with the technique of a skier: to make a good descent, we must trace your way well, and for that you must always turn before the gate, that is, we must anticipate the problem. If you do not do it that way, you will end up skipping a gate and being disqualified[98]. Another great slalom skier lesson is that we must always look forward, toward the slope. When skiing, you should never pull back, because you fall: you must face the challenge. Paquito won that gold medal against all odds and still remains to date the only Spanish skier who won a gold medal at a Winter Olympics, which is really amazing if you consider how little snow falls on the Iberian peninsula. The strategy department is responsible for setting the trace to avoid missing a gate.

We ask for some crises: they boil slowly, and we ignore their warnings. Mr. so-and-so has had a stroke; some will say how unfortunate for him, others will not say anything, but will remember that he has been smoking two packs per day for twenty years, has accumulated extra weight, and suddenly the economic crisis appeared. And it happened, even though we have

---

[97] Paquito Fernández Ochoa was a special slalom olympic champion in Sapporo on February 13, 1972.

[98] Note to young readers: The same occurs with exams and slaloms, you cannot prepare yourself at the very last minute, because you will not get it and fail.

known for a long time that smoking is not good, nor being overweight and that stress affects health and is difficult to manage. Likewise, economic crises do not come suddenly, they also warn us. You cannot be a fool. A tulip bulb cannot be worth more than a house, it is illogical, but, despite that, there were people who did exactly what the economist, Fernando Trías de Bes, explains in an essential book, which is very easy and enjoyable to read, to understand economic crises: *El hombre que cambió su casa por un tulipán* (The man who changed his home for a tulip). If you drink alcohol, do not drive. If you are not chaste, at least be cautious and use quality condoms; if not, assume that you can end up having a child with someone you have met on the boarding list of a transatlantic flight that was delayed and whom you barely know, rather do not know from anywhere at all (a true story, about which I obviously will not give any details). Judgment prevents crises. Planes do not get into a storm, they surround it, it is okay to be a little late. The problem is not arriving. It is smarter to avoid a crisis than resolving it. It is smarter to avoid a problem, if possible, than resolving it.

There is not a good harvest every year; thus, we must keep the barn full. Sometimes, there are seven years of drought. It is impossible to control everything, especially in business. You need to keep material and spiritual reserves.

Time

To overcome a crisis and its aftermath takes time. When a loved one dies, we need to go through a period of mourning, we must digest the new situation, and that takes time. A fruit only ripens with time. In such circumstances, time passes slowly. Digesting a meal takes time. After a banquet, one feels heavy and needs even more time to digest. The worse the crisis is, the more time is needed to recover: it is ok, it is that simple, and little can be done to minimize the process, but to accept reality and the mystery of life. Some things happen and are not understood.

The key to success lies in overcoming the crisis

I have extended this chapter, because I believe that the key to success in life and in all projects lies in how we face and overcome crises. They are inevitable, because we are imperfect and we live in an imperfect world, but the good news is that we have many more resources than we imagine to overcome them. We have the best resources that have ever existed throughout the history of mankind.

The key points are as follows:
- The fatigue of people and materials is very dangerous. You have to perform preventive maintenance.
- The important thing is that the plant does not blow up, that the boat does not sink, or that the spaceship does not get lost in outer space.
- Recognizing the problem and assessing its actual importance. Not overacting. Prioritizing cold analysis and reflection. If it all comes down

to a skipped slalom gate, it is better to laugh about it and try it again.

- Responding at the appropriate moment, seeking balance, the midpoint between precipitation and procrastination.
- You choose the attitude with which you face it. Remember that those who are mentally stronger will survive.
- Crises warn us; we must learn to read the signs.
- The best thing is to resolve crises in advance, to anticipate the problem, as slalom skiers do.
- We must use the appropriate technology and, as far as possible, the best one available.

You get out of a crisis reinforced. According to Winston Churchill: "Success is the ability to go from failure to failure without losing your enthusiasm."

26. Leadership in innovation processes

Leading is getting
a team to have
the right attitude.

Leading is an art. Leading an innovation and change process is even more so.

Leading means getting people to do what they have to do, because they are convinced of it; but it is not about getting results at any price nor being fully in charge, it is not about having power; it is, rather, about having authority, persuasion skills, and influence.

Lao Tse[99] is right in stating that "a leader is best when people barely know that he exists. When his work is done, his aim fulfilled, they will say, 'We did this ourselves.'" Really brilliant. This approach has many advantages, especially one: it avoids envy, one of the

> A leader
> is best when
> people barely
> know that
> he exists
> *Lao Tse*

---

[99] Lao Tse, a Chinese philosopher of the 4th century BC and author of *Tao Te Ching* (The Book of the Way and Power), the base of Taoist philosophy.

biggest risks of failure and one of the major obstacles to be overcome. The leader is the catalyst of reaction and then disappears.

It is very interesting to observe how, already at that time, intelligent people like Lao Tse advised the authorities to intervene as little as possible in the life of the people and not to burden them with taxes and regulations. I share that idea; perhaps the reader thinks that this reflection is not appropriate here, but I have not repressed myself and also think that it is relevant indeed, because a good leader needs to allow the team some space, know how to delegate, trust them; in the same way that a good political leader has to rely on their citizens, not overdo their control and treat them like criminals, when it usually goes the other way round, that the leaders are the actual criminals.

Leading innovation is being able to communicate bad news, such as that people will have to work harder and differently. The leader is the messenger who announces that they must leave the comfort zone, routine. You must know how to communicate that idea, but above all, you have to convince.

The leader needed to promote or manage an innovation process must be a Renaissance-type person, that is, a generalist, not a specialist technician. They must have an overview or at least be able to set up a team, whose members provide different viewpoints on the same challenge. Reality is, at least, a three-dimensional polyhedron, has many uneven sides. You cannot contemplate it from one standpoint alone, because a flat projection, a partial, limited vision is thus obtained. Let us look at reality from different angles and be observant. I felt highly supported in this approach when I saw that the picture of the polyhedron is also used by Pope Francis[100].

The ancient Romans distinguished between power and authority. Authority is always better than power. Power is a guiding or coercive authority. For example, state power makes you pay taxes, and, if you do not, you will get a fine and even a prison sentence. Authority, however, must be understood as prestige, credit, recognition, legitimacy based on quality, competence, knowledge about a subject. Penalizing or imposing must be the last option for a leader, who has to resort to using power only when there is no other choice; but they should not waive it, because sometimes you have to use it. When the force of reason does not work, we must, unfortunately, apply the reason of force.

Just like the bishop has a miter[101] and a staff, the leader must have wisdom and authority, but also power. The miter is not only a sign of dignity, but, above all, a sign of wisdom and knowledge. For its part, the staff is the sign of the pastor and serves to correct the lost sheep. The goal of the leader is to establish an environment of disciplined collaboration, such as Morten T. Hansen, a

> The goal of the leader is to establish an environment of disciplined collaboration

---

[100] Interview by Henrique Cymerman of Pope Francis in *La Vanguardia*, 06/13/2014.

[101] High and pointed headcloth of Jewish origin, with which Catholic and Armenian bishops, abbots, and abbesses cover their heads in liturgical ceremonies.

professor at the University of California, Berkeley, states in his book, *Collaboration*.

Projects are a serious thing, they are not a party. There is no room for mistakes, failing to observe dates, doing things halfway, errors in amounts, being late at meetings, or throwing cogs in the wheels. Unfortunately, these bad practices are permitted too many times, because whoever is at the front is a coordinator, not a leader or a person in charge, and lacks a minimum of power. Less coordinators and more directors are needed.

Someone has to grant the power, someone from above[102]: the management. The leader needs a good sponsor who supports and monitors them. We must always ask whether we have sufficient authority before hitting the stick, lest we are disavowed.

The ten best practices to lead an innovation process and which have been discussed throughout the book are as follows:

1. Involving representatives of the entire organization, starting with the most influential people, from the very beginning of the process.
2. Selling the process. Dedicating resources to market the project.
3. Listening, asking, taking time with those most directly affected by the change, accompanying them while they develop their daily work. Detecting where they have difficulties, where it hurts them.

---

[102] John 19, 11: "You would have no authority over Me, unless it had been given you from above."

4. The analysis and design stages are critical. Designs must not only be accurate and correct, but, above all, simple.
5. Knowing how to manage meetings. Watch out for large meetings, problems must be solved in advance. Agreements are reached before starting the meetings.
6. Prioritizing one-by-one contacts. Be careful with email. It is more convenient to use the phone or, even better, still make video calls. Always improve your own communication skills. Having a beer, a coffee, or a glass of wine at the right moment helps.
7. Be very strict about testing systems in the laboratory and in an actual situation. Quality control is very important. Perform load and stress tests.
8. Training should not be left for the very last moment, because it helps to sell an innovation. Education, selling, setting up an innovative system should run parallel to the project development and must be refreshed later.
9. Adjust the solution. Excellence can be found in the details: you have to fine-tune adjustments.
10. Celebrate the project completion, take a short break, and start again.

The person in charge of a project or an innovative process should be as follows
- Renaissance-type.
- Good communicator.
- Good negotiator.
- Innovative and imaginative.

- Able to delegate.
- Good at listening.
- Able to link differently in knowledge, technologies, and insights.
- A little bad-tempered and moderately rude.

27. Information and communications technologies

To survive and succeed
in life you need networks.

Throughout the book we have repeatedly stressed the importance of communication for any activity to be successful, without ever hiding the intrinsic difficulty of human communication. For those reasons and also out of professional bias, I will devote a chapter to explain, while avoiding technical aspects, the evolution of communication technologies and to present the available tools. Being aware of this challenge, we should not give up using all means available, including technical ones.

We cannot afford the typical excuse of politicians, especially when they justify with apparent conviction their umpteenth electoral failure: "We have failed to communicate our ideas." In real life, you must not only know how to communicate, but you should also have a good message and credibility. Unlike politicians, if we do not communicate well, we will not eat.

Why, if we are familiar with the difficulties of human communication, do we give up using the technical means that facilitate it? For example, why do we force customers, who want to contact us, to use the channel that interests us and not one which they feel comfortable with? What technical means and solutions do we have at our disposal?

The network concept

A network is a powerful concept. Eleven are the meanings of that term offered by the dictionary of the Royal Spanish Academy[103]. Among them, I think the most appropriate one is the seventh meaning: "Set of organized elements for a particular purpose." Let us analyze for how many things a network is used:

- To eat; we still fish with nets.
- To protect us.
- To rescue someone.
- To communicate; we refer to railway, shipping, communications, telecommunications networks.
- To think; our most powerful organ, the brain, is a network of neurons which are connected together.

In English, the same term is used, *networking,* to refer to a computer network and the network of personal and professional contacts. This term has already imposed itself and is now a universal concept.

Social networks allow you to maintain and resume contacts with many people whom, previously, we would have definitely lost. Furthermore, they allow you to contact, discuss, and exchange information with people with similar interests. The networking community, Internet forums solve problems.

To survive and succeed in life, networks are needed. Let us see what we have available to build and use them.

---

[103] lema.rae.es/drae/?val=red

Converging networks and unified communications

As a proud citizen of Barcelona, I am going to base my account on one of the fundamental ideas of Antoni Gaudí to try to explain how the current communications networks look like. The great architect, author of the world-famous Basilica of the Sagrada Familia[104], sought inspiration in nature, which is God's creation and the environment in which problems have been best resolved. We are going to use this forceful idea and rely on an anthropomorphic model to explain the new tools in communication technologies.

Let us observe ourselves, our own body. How does our communications system work? How does our brain work? Our body's communication system is the nervous system. We have a single system that transports various types of sign, voice, video, touch, temperature, etc. from different sensors to the brain. We have an integrated communications system. To make a decision, the data center, the brain, processes and interrelates all the information coming from different sources. The brain is conveniently protected by a bony structure, the skull. Servers must also be located in a suitable enclosure. Until

> The nervous system is our body's communications network

---

[104] www.sagradafamilia.cat

a few years ago, all telecommunications systems were isolated, that is to say, there was a telephone network (voice), a data network, a video streaming network, and a TV network. Each part required specific equipment. With converging networks using a single protocol (IP or Internet Protocol), we have finally reached a solution which is equivalent to nature: a single network that transmits voice, data, image, and control signs. A new generation of computer applications is going to be developed that can process simultaneously those different kinds of information. We have a good solution, inspired by nature, and it opens up countless opportunities for improvement.

The unstoppable expansion of mobile networks, both in terms of coverage and communication capacities, have broken the physical limitations of the workplace. The limits of the office, hospital, factory are surpassed. We are, if we so desire, permanently connected and accessing the information we require at all times.

Very schematically, we can say that we are able to capture any type of information in real time, at the place where it originates, transport it to the processing center, where established rules and procedures are applied, and deliver it processed to the right person, wherever they are at that specific moment. On these powerful communication networks, which are reliable and inexpensive, grouped tools are run under the generic name of Unified

> Thanks to mobile communications, the office's walls have fallen

Communications and Collaboration (UC2), which manage all communications: voice and data, fixed and mobile, throughout the entire organization.

My friend, colleague, and international reference, Marty Parker[105], teaches us that implementing unified communications in an organization means to introduce the new communication methods as an additional component of the task sequence of a business process in order to make the process more efficient, that is to say, for the task to be performed correctly and successfully, without wasting any time or energy. For this purpose, we use parts that worked separately in the past and integrate them, as we need the process efficiency to meet the challenges we encounter (as already discussed in earlier chapters). We must improve productivity, if we want to compete, that is, we must do things better and with less effort. According to Parker: "Integrated communications to optimize business processes." It is worth analyzing each of those terms.

- "Communications" refers to the technology that facilitates interaction between people via voice, image, and text.
- "Integrated" means that they are built into the business process.
- "Optimize" means being more efficient.
- "Business processes" are the sequence of inter-related tasks aimed at achieving a business result, such as a sale.

---

[105] www.ucstrategies.com/unified-communications-strategies-experts/marty-parker.aspx

The processes that occur in a company can be either regular events or incidents and alarms. Thanks to the UC2 tools and the integration between communications and computer systems they provide, we can automate these two types of processes to reduce their life cycle and avoid errors. The key word is process and its corresponding workflow or flowchart. Flows are automated and optimized.

By way of example, we are going to discuss a telemetry and alarm management application at a hospital. We have the patient monitoring equipment connected to the network and communications server. When an incident occurs, the system automatically alerts the nurse on duty via a message that appears on the chosen communication device or even on several at the same time. The nurse must acknowledge the message and act according to the protocol they have set. The whole process is recorded. There is no need for a person in a control room to wait for an incident to happen nor to rely on someone hearing a beep. The results of implementing an alarm management which is integrated with communications are spectacular. Research carried out by Philips Healthcare in the United States under the direction of Michael Breslow (which was presented at the e-Health Conference in Barcelona in March 2010[106]) concludes that the use of telemetry systems reduces mortality by 20% in intensive care units and by 30% patient hospitalization time. "The data show that 90% of interventions from remote equipment—Breslow points out—correspond

---

[106] www.hospitecnia.com/Servicios-Hospitalarios/Noticias/telemedicina-integrada-con-los/id-Lbfjdjaihcehdde.xsql

to problems identified by that equipment, not by professionals on the bedside. Besides, said remote equipment caters to routine tasks, in case the ICU professionals cannot, so much so that you can cover more than one hundred patients with an intensivist and two nurses."

Another simple example of how you can get great savings in a hospital environment is the introduction of a one-time medication schedule in real time. If three hundred medical visits to patients are done every day at a hospital and the doctor sets the medication schedules or instructions for the nursing staff directly on the system rather than on paper, besides avoiding transcription errors, the administrative process of introducing again the data in the systems is removed. This simple change can represent savings of five minutes per patient and prescription, which in one year amount to 9,125 hours of administrative work.

Telelocalizing of equipment and people within the hospital premises allows you to always know where they are, ensuring their protection and swift availability.

Network collaboration

In this network of interconnected neurons that the brain is, the more connections there are, the more developed it is, and the more knowledge and skills the person has. Similarly, converging high-capacity IP networks allow you to create networking teams, multidisciplinary and multicultural groups with high potential, though their members are geographically apart. Multi video conference platforms and collaboration tools enable multipoint video calls from the workplace and sharing documents or whiteboards in real time with very low costs. Obviously, a face-to-face meeting is not the same as a meeting using telepresence, but the fact is that non-personal meetings allow you to reduce a lot of travels. The fact of avoiding a journey to a meeting has highly important direct and indirect cost savings: lost hours, transport costs, allowances, and fatigue, among other factors.

Networking fosters the development of project work. Teams that are created expressly for particular projects and that are dissolved as soon as the objectives set are achieved and who do not have to work in the same geographic location. Flexible structures versus rigid organizations. Stephen Covey explains this from another point of view: he considers that a person is highly effective when they are interdependent and able to collaborate with others to create wealth and achieve more ambitious goals.

This very model would include the concept of working at home. ICT tools allow for many tasks to be completed at home instead of having to move to a workplace. To be in front of a computer and a phone you do not need to move; it is the case, for example, of an agent at a multimedia customer care center. An interesting variant of homeworking is working at shared centers (coworking), [107]which are located close to home, where freelancers and people from different organizations work; this solves the disadvantage of

---

[107] www.coworkingspain.es

possible loneliness and lack of space in your private dwelling. You do not have to lose two to three hours a day in traffic, wasting gas, paying two hundred euros (or dollars) per month for downtown parking, or despair on a commuter train. The reconciliation of work and family or personal life is a challenge we cannot evade. We cannot go on living at this pace. A good business model easily demonstrates the economic and social profitability of these solutions.

Multimedia and multichannel interaction centers

A multimedia interaction center is a center which is equipped to deal not only with phone calls, but also with video calls, chats, emails, and shared or directed Internet browsing. A website should be part of the interaction center, as it is a form of communication with customers; it cannot be a mere catalog (that was the first version) nor is it enough if it is integrated with social networks (Web 2.0). Web 3.0 interacts with the client, who, upon accessing, is invited to chat, call, we let them know that we are at their disposal for whatever they may need. It is a website with a human touch in real time, as people not only interact with a machine.

Meanwhile, WebRTC solutions[108] will provide even more communication capacity and closer integration between websites and communications in real time.

---

[108] *WebRTC for Enterprises: History and Use Cases.* Christopher J. Vitek and Philip E. Edholm. www.webrtcstrategies.com

For the first time in history, innovation reaches first the private and domestic spheres than businesses. For the generation of the new millennium, our children, ICTs are not new, because they already existed when they were born and they have always lived with them. Companies lag behind and will have a communication problem with their future customers and employees. We must incorporate the new communication channels in organizations. How many multimedia customer interaction centers do you know?

Mobility

Mobility is another major challenge in corporate communications. Providing the mobile workforce with access to the integrated voice, data, and video network is the most important action that can be undertaken to improve their productivity. With 3G and 4G data connections, you can be permanently connected to the company systems and make many inquiries and transactions in real time. You do not have to go home or to the hotel at night and connect to the Internet. Other applications which are related to mobility and are highly profitable are those of localization fleet management, and route optimization.

Decreasing the process life cycle through, for example, the availability of information in real time represents major savings. How much is the increase in customer satisfaction worth if we instantly resolve one of their incidents? What savings does reducing a product sales cycle from days to minutes represent?

Clouds

And is it very difficult to enjoy all these tools in a company? Do we need to have highly specialized technicians and invest a lot of money?

Although nothing is free and easy, it is neither very difficult nor expensive to enjoy all these solutions, as they can be hired in the cloud on a pay-per-use basis. In the same way that you do not need to have a power plant to enjoy electricity, currently, many of the information technology and communications solutions do not require equipment to be installed at a company's physical office, as they are in the cloud, or rather, in the Web. In addition, as-a-service models allow you to overcome the brake on innovation which represents the fact of having to bear the investment costs. The challenge is to understand well what you need and, therefore, what the appropriate solutions are depending on the characteristics of each organization. That is, value lies in process analysis and design.

Cloud services have the great advantage that the technical aspects, which are really complex and cumbersome, are borne by suppliers, and businesses can focus their efforts on what provides them actual value. The supplier is responsible for the system to work and that it is correctly sized and updated. Meanwhile, the user focuses on running their business and on defining the functionality of technological tools.

The term "cloud" is wrong; it is a marketing mistake. We associate clouds with storms, thunder, and lightning; when clouds are close to the ground and you get into one of them, you are surrounded by fog and cannot see anything. It is a term with too many negative connotations. We would have to say that they are services that are on the web (on the net) and that we can reach through it. In fact, many other vital services, such as water supply, electricity, or gas, are also in the cloud.

Being in the cloud has a humongous advantage: anywhere with web (Internet) access, by cable or radio, and having electricity (or batteries in portable devices), you can enjoy the services, access to information, and any type of communications.

The main distrust generated by this type of data storage is not knowing where the data is and the fear that they are accessible to anyone who should not, or else that they get lost. We are obviously relying on the company that provides the service, on its security systems, on its employees, and that both will abide by the law. However, if we analyze it objectively, we must also see what security systems are implemented in many companies, especially SMEs, how backups are made, what access control and user authentication systems are implemented, and in whose hands lies the whole process. Often only a few people or a single person is responsible for all that, which is poorly documented, whereas the risk that any incident might happen to the person in charge or even that they may be disloyal is not valued.

Let us take a simple example: maintaining an updated contact agenda is a nuisance, people change company or the company changes its name, location, email, etc. With a traditional home agenda, after a few months, if you do not have regular contact with a person, the chances to find them quickly decrease.

However, if contacts are established on LinkedIn, for example, each one of them thinks about keeping their data updated, whereas much more information is also accessible about the person, their employment or academic history, groups they participate in, etc., information which, incidentally, does not violate any complex and puritanical data protection law, as each one of us is free to complete the profile as they see fit and be part of the social network or not. That is, having your agenda on LinkedIn is more efficient and provides more information and is more reliable, and less effort is required to keep it updated. Nevertheless, it is good to have a copy in another cloud service or on your own computer, because you never know what can happen.

Big Data

At present, many and highly varied data sources are generated and stored, which, if properly processed, provide a wealth of information. Techniques such as technology watch and competitive intelligence or data mining, among others, offer great opportunities.

For example, telecom operators, through statistics from cellular phone records, may know the flows of people in specific cities. In Barcelona, we have analyzed how tourists move around the city according to their nationalities and have established patterns. It turns out that Russian, Japanese, and American tourists do not visit the same sights, and astonishing data points are obtained, such as the high percentage of cruise passengers arriving at Barcelona who do not leave the ship; to be more precise, what we know is that they connect their cellular phone and the latter, the terminal, does not leave the ship. Given that Barcelona is one of the most highly valued tourist destinations on the planet, the data is sobering, and Barcelona Tourism will have to get moving on this matter, because we need tourists to leave the comfort of the ship and stroll around and spend a few euros in the city.

Technology is not a commodity

The bursting of the dotcom bubble and various scams[109] have conveyed to society the message that all this can be a bluff. The idea has even spread that the Internet is a game, an entertainment, in some cases even highly dangerous. These impressions and messages have masked a reality, which is that the Internet has consolidated itself and that information technology and telecommunications converge and that bandwidth grows exponentially and so does the ability to transmit information.

The top management has gone from being directly involved in decision-making as regards information technology to almost ignoring the issue. The tools we have discussed allow very significant business re-engineering to be carried out. They are strategic decisions. We have come to think that technology is

---

[109] Example: Gowex.

234

a commodity[110], that it is not a differentiating factor; a big mistake: not using the right solution or the best option to perform a task makes a big difference, in the same way that using spears instead of tanks has consequences or that it is not the same if you use a cart pulled by mules to transport goods or a truck. You can do your job with both options, but it is obvious that one way is more efficient than the other. The important thing is to realize that choosing the correct and appropriate technology is an activity for the senior management. In Covey's time management model, this is an activity within the second quadrant, that is, it is important but not urgent: It is strategic. In his argumentation, Covey concludes that one of the results obtained with such activities is that fewer crises occur.

---

[110] I use the term commodity, because its meaning implies it is just that and does not provide a differential or an added value. It is used in a derogatory manner.

Part IV

CONCLUSIONS.
THE LIFE CYCLE

28. The servo system

*It is essential
to adjust the process
depending on the outcome.*

Miguel Ramírez, the first dean of the Catalan Telecommunication Engineers Association, was my college professor on servo systems. I remember our first day of class, when he blurted that the best servo system ever invented was the toilet chain. The process is adapted depending on the outcome. The water flow entering the tank is controlled, depending on the level the water is reaching, until it stops, when it has attained its full capacity, before overflowing. The filling process is restarted when the tank is completely empty.

A servo system is a mechanical, electromechanical, electrical, or electronic system that regulates itself as soon as it detects an error or a difference between its actual and its desired performance, and which maintains the desired result by instantly correcting any deviation from its normal operation.

This is the very same concept we should apply to the rules that govern society, as well as to the products and services provided by a company. If we do not get the expected results—the creation of jobs and wealth, an increase of sales and benefits—, we must change the processes and adjust the rules of the game, because what matters are the results, not the rules.

We must accept that we do not always obtain the same results, even if we maintain the procedures we have always used, as there are countless factors that influence the results and not all of them can be covered by procedures; thus, it is necessary to control the results and question them.

It is not easy to change a process, but the worst thing of all is that we often do not even consider the need nor the possibility of tackling a change. The natural thing is to admit that monitoring (observing and assessing) the results and questioning the process are an intrinsic part of the process itself: that is what the concept of servo system implies.

A servo system is a circle which guarantees the correctness of the results: it is a virtuous circle.

The project methodology we have discussed is a servo system. Many other decision-making and process development methods are as well. Below we will discuss the aforementioned OODA loop by Colonel Boyd and suggest others, but each person and each company must develop their own and adapt them to their own circumstances to, eventually, acquire

Figure 4. OODA loop by John Boyd.

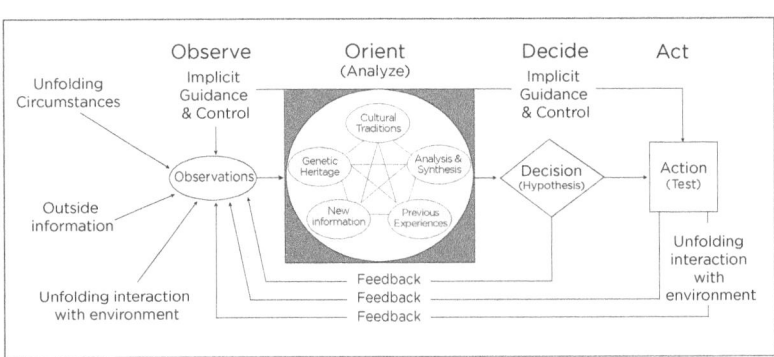

them as a habit and apply them unconsciously and intuitively.

As shown in Figure 4, OODA is clearly a servo system. What I like about this method of swift decision-building, designed for fighter pilots, but which can be applied to almost every field, is the fact that it contemplates interaction with the environment and, after collecting external information, feeds back at all process stages. It relies on four points:

1. **Observation.** We must observe the current situation, including the circumstances that surround us. The quality of observation is crucial to the the model's success and generates more reliable and effective decisions.

2. **Orientation.** Once we know the reality which we are immersed in, we try to focus by thinking and using the knowledge, experience, results of analysis and synthesis, as well as comparative studies we have been accumulating.

3. **Decision.** With all the accumulated information and its analysis, we must choose an alternative, Boyd calls it a "hypothesis." Let us recall that Boyd designed his model for supersonic military aircraft pilots; thus, you have to be skillful and fast both in generating options and in choosing one of them, which gives us a competitive advantage.

4. **Action.** When the decision has already been implemented, the outcome must be observed and incorporated into the first stage, that is, you start again, but with more information.

A similar loop to Boyd's is called CECA: Critique-Explore-Compare-Adapt, developed by the Canadian

Figure 5. Continuous improvement by repeating the Shewhart/ Deming cycle.

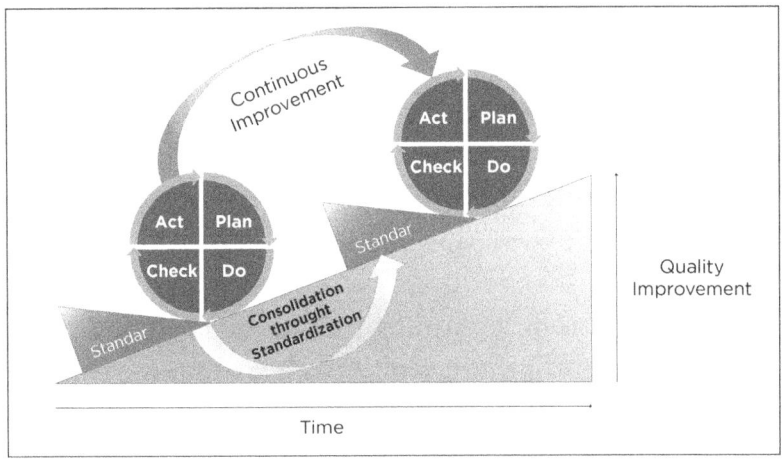

David Bryant, also a military researcher, and published by the Defence Research and Development Center of the Government of Canada.[111.]

Boyd was not the first person to suggest such ideas, and there are many similar models that are not from a military environment; especially the so-called Shewhart/Deming quality control cycle[112] stands out, identified as PDCA and summarized in Plan-Do-Check-Act (Adjust), as the outcome will differ from the desired results.

---

[111] www.drdc-rddc.gc.ca

[112] Walter Andrew Shewhart and William Edwards Deming are American engineers and mathematicians specializing in quality control and continuous improvement. Deming was inspired by Shewhart's work and had a great influence on the reconstruction of the Japanese industry after World War II. www.deming.org

It is important to emphasize that all these methods suggest to be repeated over and over again; it is about taking on a continued commitment to a specific subject, as we improve based on persistence and insistence. We move on by consolidating what we have learned each time we executed the loop, as shown in Figure 5. Deming teaches us that we consolidate what we have learned when we standardize it.

All models contain common sense and none of these examples teaches us anything we do not know, but it is good to have them to understand, even if only partially, how the world works.

Continuously enhancing the creative process

With no relation to engineering, Mario Alonso Puig suggests a technique or methodology to enhance the creative process and bring out our best version: Stretch-Relax-Wait-Trust.

- **Stretch.** Work, read, reflect, study, analyze.
- **Relax.** Rest, walk, stop brooding on the issue you are concerned about.
- **Wait and trust.** The brain will eventually find the best solution.

I dare suggest that we repeatedly perform the creative process Mario Alonso Puig teaches us, completing it with a fourth point, the analysis of results, and add that analysis to the start of the next creative process, the next *stretch,* so that it becomes a habit, is repeated again and again, turns into a continuum; once a challenge or issue has been solved, let us tackle the following, so as not to be complacent with the first and only great idea we had, as the founders of BlackBerry did.

The continuous improvement cycle I suggest, which can be applied to the development of any type of business or life project, or solving a problem or challenge, is as follows:

- Asking oneself. Questioning whether we are doing it well, why we do it this way, and if it can be improved.
- Finding information.
- Thinking and reflecting on the matter.
- Relating and describing possible alternatives.
- Comparing options.
- Choosing *(making* a decision).
- Designing in detail the chosen solution and the action plan.
- Acting.
- Analyzing the results.
- Making the necessary adjustments.
- Enjoy the success. Celebrate it.
- Take a rest or some vacations.
- Not settling for it. Questioning reality again. Comparing how the world is like and how we would like it to be.
- Restarting, asking ourselves again the same or other questions.

29. Intelligent communities and organizations

The rules of the game in our society should not be an unsolvable equation to drown us.

At the conference of the Canadian Telecommunications Consultants Association in Ottawa, held in May 2011, I was able to get in touch with the concept of *smart community* through the presentation of the consultant, William G. Hutchison[113], who is a member of the Intelligent Community Forum[114] and president of the Canadian Advanced Technology Alliance[115], which promote and develop this concept.

The proposal of this group, which is summarized in Figure 6, goes far beyond a smart city, a concept which focuses more on city automation. An intelligent community is one in which an environment or ecosystem of mutual collaboration has been created that enables the creation of a good place to live, work, learn, and even entertain oneself. The collaboration ecosystem is based on creating an excited community, an optimistic environment that encourages and facilitates innovation and creativity. This requires providing the

---

[113] www.hutchison-management.com

[114] www.intelligentcommunity.org

[115] www.cata.ca

community with adequate infrastructures which are adapted to the environment, where the community is located, and which, of course, must be sustainable; amongst others, it is considered essential to invest in ultra-broadband communication networks with a huge transmission capacity. In this collaborative environment and with adequate infrastructures, a set of applications would be developed as a basis for regular wealth creation:

- i-Health (health and healthcare).
- i-Education (education).
- i-Government (government).
- i-Community (community and coexistence improvement).
- i-Business (business).
- i-Arts & Entertainment (culture and entertainment).

Figure 6. Intelligent Community Open Architecture Tasting Model.

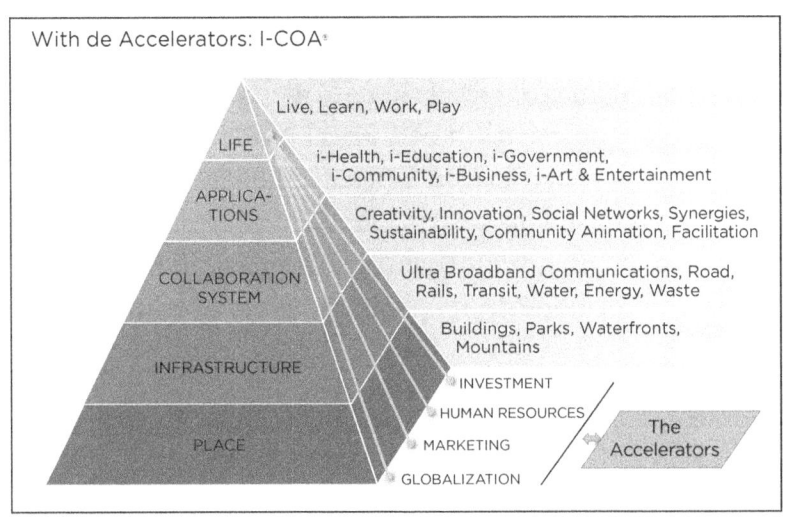

Analogous to a community, an intelligent organization or company should also create a collaborative environment that promotes cooperation between the different company divisions and between its employees, in order to break the isolated silos that are set up inside, as well as the trend to compete rather than collaborate among them. The aim is for the company to be a suitable place for the development and growth of individuals through continuous learning and the satisfaction and recognition for a job well done.

The features of a smart organization would be as follows:

- Cutting-edge technological infrastructures in the cloud. They must be hyperconnected.
- Disciplined collaboration. Use of collaborative tools, also called "universal communications."
- Learning organization. An organization which learns every day.
- Networking by project, in a multidisciplinary, multicultural environment, and with the participation of external partners that complement the team.
- Aligned with a shared goal, from the property (shareholders) to the employees, through the management.
- Efficient working procedures, as simple as possible, and permanently being adjusted and renewed.
- Minimum bureaucratic structure.
- It must have a strategy and competitive intelligence department.

An intelligent community is that which is governed by rules of the game that generate wealth and conveniently adapts them to the circumstances and evolving times, not those who have built an unsolvable equation or an unworkable system of bureaucratic rules which block everything and only serve as protection for entrenched parasites.

30. The life cycle

The king is dead,
long live the king.

Life is a circle. Let us observe nature: each year, we work, fertilize the soil, sow, irrigate, harvest, and again work the land. After each winter, spring comes, and then summer and fall, and thus one year after another, but none is equal to the preceding one. It is the cycle of life, constant renewal, continuous innovation. Wondering, thinking, and meditating, finding the best solution, locating and defining alternatives, comparing options, choosing *(making* a decision), designing the action plan in detail, acting, analyzing the results, making the necessary adjustments, and starting over.

Life without a transcendent vision and lacking goals is like a sine wave propagating, with peaks and valleys, but tending to dampen. The proposal is to turn it into an upward spiral, a spiral of improvement, a virtuous spiral, which increasingly spans more knowledge and creativity, hence generating more wealth, be it material or spiritual.

You have to get the right rhythm, as the cyclist, Miguel Indurain, did, the winner of five Tours de France, who seemed to climb mountains unfazed, with a regular pedaling cadence and without hitting the wall. A completely different style was exhibited by another great cyclist, Perico Delgado, the winner of one Tour, who rushed off in such a precipitous manner at the beginning of a pass, hence generating unrestrained excitement with television commentators, but who often ran out of oxygen halfway up the slope, full of passion and courage as he was; he won a Tour, but not five like his friend Indurain. You have to reach a good pace for best results. Indurain was less passionate, but cooler and smarter[116].

This world works based on a strange balance; when we take a medicine, we must take the right dose; if we take little of it, we will not get better, and if we take too much of it, we poison ourselves. The same thing happens with hormones: If the concentration of one of them is lower than necessary, it is a bad thing, but if we generate too many, it is not good either. If we fall into fundamentalism and do not think, we are faring badly; if we move along without any values, we will not work well either. If we only want rights, but no obligation, we are imbalanced. We need the right amount of positive stress. We are unable to work with an excessively protected society, but we cannot fall into the law of the jungle either. We must find the balance between the two tendencies of mankind, the pursuit of excellence and the pursuit of pleasure.

We are runners in a relay race, not one of a hundred or four hundred meters taking place in an Olympic stadium, but rather a distance race, in which we receive the baton from the generation preceding us and we deliver it to the one replacing us. The important thing is that we deliver a better baton than the one we have received, and that is within our reach. That our

---

[116] It is remarkable how Perico has turned into an excellent sports commentator.

children are better than us and live in a better world. It is in our hands, if we act wisely, rest a bit, and act again once we have observed the results.

Let us convince ourselves that we need to innovate to solve the crisis, which means changing or modifying something by introducing something new, adapting it to the circumstances of each specific moment. To innovate we have at our disposal philosophical, organizational, and technological tools that allow us to create more efficient procedures and solutions. It is not about being able to use them; we already know that we can, we are reminded of that all day long with the famous slogan, *yes, we can*; what matters is that we must use them. Do we really want to change and continuously improve? Let us replace the *yes, we can* sentence with *yes, we want to*.

"We choose to go to the moon," that is what really matters, making the right decision and acting. There is no alternative to not acting, because waiting, delaying decisions, and ignoring reality is not going to get us out of the crisis. Dying of starvation is not funny, let us at least die with our boots on. We must choose to act, choose to innovate, decide to improve, want to strive. What are we waiting for? Now that the speculative economy is over, were are back to an economy of realities, of values, not of prices, to the economy of effort, of the virtuous cycle of continuous improvement.

There is no alternative: constant improvement and progress or deterioration and decrepitude the Cuban way.

The best challenge and the greatest opportunity are yet to come. Let us believe in it and let us get started now. Let us be tenacious. We count on you.

Clear and distinct ideas.
Quick impact list

If you do not have time or do not feel like reading the whole book, or if, after finishing it, you want a quick reminder, I have summarized the most important ideas or concepts that have been covered throughout these pages in the form of mottos. I guess American publicists call this technique bullets. I copied this idea from the quick impact list in the book, *The Trusted Advisor*, by David H. Maister[117], a text all professional consultants should read.

1. The challenge
   - To solve a problem you must first acknowledge and accept it.
   - The real crisis is the crisis of values.
   - Malthus and his disciples—who are quite numerous—are wrong, because they deny innovation. They predict disasters regardless of the improvements and discoveries we are continuously making.
   - Reality is polyhedral (multifaceted).

2. Obstacles and barriers
   - The worst laziness is the mental one.
   - We may encounter: builders, destroyers, and vegetating people.

---

[117] *The Trusted Advisor*, David H. Maister, Charles H. Green, and Robert M. Galford. Free Press, NY, 2000.

- Be careful, there is always someone who scores his own goals.
- Envy is highly destructive. Envious people seek lose-lose agreements.
- Doing nothing is almost never a good solution.
- True wellbeing is being satisfied with yourself, not having it all sorted.
- We are not freer if we do not commit ourselves. We do not progress without committing ourselves.
- Make a phone call. Or, rather, make a video call.
- Emails are dangerous, you never know where they end.
- Prioritize one-by-one contacts.

3. Tools
   - We have many very good tools to face the problems.
   - We have never had so much great technology.
   - We know ourselves and other human beings increasingly better.
   - Attitude is a personal choice and cannot be bought. Instead, skills (aptitudes) can be acquired or hired.
   - What are we excited about each morning?
   - Let us be influential, do not remain silent.
   - Do not take decisions, *make* them.
   - Let us keep the division of powers; at least three legs are needed to support a structure.
   - It is okay to ask what we do not know.

- We need people working on important but not urgent things: in the analysis and strategy department.
- Innovations and changes have to be sold, and this is difficult.
- Good agreements are win-win ones.
- Good contracts are those which are left rotting in drawers.
- Learning organization: a culture of continuous learning.
- Beware of meetings. Prepare them thoroughly.
- The key to success of projects is found at the analysis and design stage.
- Keep it simple. Simplify.
- You have to carry out load tests and a whole array of tests before implementing a new system.
- Celebrate successes, share them.
- A leader is best when people barely know that he exists.
- A good leader gets his team to adopt the right attitude and collaborate with discipline.
- The world is imperfect, and there are unforeseen events and misfortunes.
- When a crisis strikes: react and cool down.
- Communication networks are the nervous system of the organization; if they do not work well, the latter will suffer from Parkinson's disease.

4. Conclusions
   - Less competition and more cooperation.

- Let us build intelligent communities that adapt their rules of the game depending on the outcome.
- You cannot stop, at most rest awhile to sharpen the saw.
- It is better to move at a regular pace than stumbling; in the way Indurain did rather than Perico Delgado.
- Balances that cannot be broken:
  o Freedom/responsibility.
  o Rights/obligations.
  o Supervision/autonomy.
  o Rewarding those who take on risks/social awareness.
- We take over from the generation preceding us and deliver it to that following us.

A success story – Mercabarna's telecommunication network

Introduction

Many of the ideas and concepts presented in this book have been applied during the development of the telecommunication network project of the Barcelona Food Unit, Mercabarna[118], where the wholesale markets of fruits and vegetables, fish and flowers, as well as the slaughterhouse, are headquartered. This unit serves more than ten million inhabitants, where about twenty-five thousand people work; it covers an area of over two hundred acres in the free trade zone and eleven acres on the new Mercabarna Airport premises.

Mercabarna is a reference center for the distribution of fresh and perishable foodstuffs, a market of global reach, where things are bought and sold worldwide. The project started in October 1992, at the end of the Barcelona Olympic Games, and is still developing and growing.

It is not that we who participated in the project had thought at the time to apply these criteria; we just used common sense, a positive view, and the will to collaborate and cooperate.

The Mercabarna project is a success and an example of innovation in different aspects:

---

[118] www.mercabarna.es

- It is an example of collaboration between the public sector and private initiative. In this case, a publicly-owned company works closely with nearly eight hundred private companies that are settled on the premises and represented by sectoral business associations: regarding fruits and vegetables, fish, flowers, and meat. The companies, many of them competing with each other, work together to achieve a common goal.
- A continuous innovation, renewal, and improvement policy is applied not only with regard to technological infrastructures, but also services are expanded and renewed and, what is more difficult, the economic and management model is adapted to the changing environment. The project began before the liberalization of the telecommunications sector.
- The use of new technologies among small and medium-sized companies from sectors that are apparently not at all technological in nature is continuously promoted. When the project was presented at a world telecommunications consulting and engineering conference in 2006, the moderator insisted on giving the session the following title: "21st-Century Information Technology Solutions for 18th-Century Businesses."[119] Every year training and promotion sessions regarding new solutions and applications are held.

---

[119] www.slideshare.net/Arging/mercabarna-case-study

- It is a long-term project, which is already over twenty years old, eighteen of which are still in operation.
- Although throughout the project there have been changes in the management team, the good aspects of the project have always been valued, while a new vision and a renewed hope are provided that enriches it.

Technical project summary

Issues

Wholesalers and buyers at Mercabarna need to be permanently connected with their foreign and domestic suppliers and customers for them to be able to search, buy, and sell foodstuffs. For proper market operation, these communications must be agile, the short expiration date of fresh food sold at Mercabarna requiring fast decision-making. For this reason, it is utterly important to have a really powerful and competitive fixed and mobile telephony service, as well as a data network and Internet access.

Objectives

From a technical point of view, the specific project objectives are as follows:
- Resolving Mercabarna's communication needs, both within and without the enclosure itself.
- Providing a competitive advantage to companies that have settled there with regard to others

that are located on other industrial estates by facilitating access to the latest information and telecommunications technology solutions.

- Setting up a powerful group of telecommunications users that allows them to enjoy the best services at the most competitive prices.

In other words, facilitating appropriate telecommunications networks and systems to support the market operations, as well as to manage the enclosure itself.

Project stages and resources used

The project, which was led by the Industrial and Services Management, was started in 1992 and is still developing.

Since the first stage of preliminary studies to date, Mercabarna has relied on the support by Argelich Networks[120], which has rendered the engineering and independent consulting services needed. Argelich has taken on the design and management of the different project stages and collaborated in establishing the network operation model and agreements with operators, system integrators, and technological equipment manufacturers.

As technology partners, leading companies in their different fields are included, such as Orange, Cisco, Siemens, Tyco Electronics (AMP), and Sony.

---

[120] www.argelich.com

The project milestones up to now are summarized below:

- 4th quarter of 1992. First feasibility studies.
- 2nd quarter of 1993. Preliminary studies are finished. Due to the subsequent economic crisis after the1992 events, the installation start is delayed.
- 1st quarter of 1996. Agreement between Mercabarna and the fruits and vegetables guild to relaunch the project.
- January 1997. Operational as internal network, without connections to the external world, stage I for the fruit and vegetable market.
- December 1997. First public network interconnection agreement with Global One, a company of the France Telecom group.
- 1st quarter of 1998. Stage II: network of the sea side complementary activities area.
- December 1998. Creation of the closed mobile telephony user group with Vodafone.
- 1st quarter of 1999. Stage III: flower market, slaughterhouse, and accesses to the premises.
- 1st quarter of 2000. Stage IV: network of the hill side complementary activities area.
- 2nd quarter of 2000. Agreement with Al-Pi (now Orange) as a network manager and fixed telephony operator.
- 3rd quarter of 2002. Stage V: fish market network.
- 2nd quarter of 2004. Migration of the Ethernet network. Replacement of hubs with Cisco switch equipment.

- 1st quarter of 2005. Wi-Fi wireless network with 160 antennas with Cisco equipment.
- 2nd quarter of 2006. Safety video using IP Video (160 cameras) with Sony.
- October 2006. Project presentation at the International Conference of the Society of Telecommunications Consultants in San Francisco.
- 1st quarter of 2007. Implementation of VoIP extensions.
- April 2008. Project presentation at the Conference of the World Union of Wholesale Markets in Mexico City.
- 1st quarter of 2009. Expansion of the new flower market on the Mercabarna Airport premises.
- 2nd quarter of 2009. New agreement to provide mobile telephony services with Orange. Enhancement of mobility services that reach four thousand mobile communication services.
- 1st quarter of 2011. Implementation of a unified communications platform and collaboration with Siemens Enterprise Networks (now Unify) for four thousand users.
- 1st quarter of 2013. Nine thousand subscriptions for mobile communications are achieved.
- 1st quarter of 2014. Replacement and renewal of core switches and firewall equipment.

The network is supported by a fiber optic infrastructure that interconnects all site buildings, complemented with category VII structured cabling. A powerful wire (100/1,000 Mbits) and wireless (Wi-Fi at 54 Mbits) Ethernet data network transmits voice, data, and image using IP protocols. Both networks, wired (cable) and wireless (radio, no cable), are equipped with sophisticated and reliable safety systems, both from the physical (element redundancy) and logical point of view (encryption, user authentication, tunneling, VLAN, VPN, etc.). The network features Internet links at redundant 1 Gbit.

A worldwide reference

The companies based at Mercabarna boast highly advanced telecommunication services with extremely competitive costs. As Lluís Alberich, manager of the Mercabarna Industrial and Service Area, points out "the fact of being integrated in a cluster, such as Mercabarna, either as an operator or as a buyer, creates great advantages for users, who have a high bargaining power against the telecommunications operator, and this allows them to gain significant benefits." Thus, tools are made available that provide profitability and productivity, whereas costs are limited while incorporating technological advances.

Undoubtedly, its ongoing investment in telecommunications is also contributing to Mercabarna's success, which has turned this organization into a world reference in its sector. The market is networking, a network of personal and business relationships and contacts, which becomes highly fluent and efficient thanks to advanced electronic networking.

The telecommunications network is Mercabarna's nervous system.

Assessment of international conferences

Below you will find an overview of the assessments issued by the "Moving Forward" conference attendees, which was given by the author at the conference of the Society of Communications Consultants in Orlando, Florida, in October 2011.[121]

- Good lessons for life. I enjoyed the different perspective!
- Very creative, as always.
- Agustín does it very well, both his English and his presentation. He has many values to share.
- A good test of the best business practices, as well as of the less good ones.
- Excellent.
- Agustín's examples are priceless. Moreover, it was fun.
- Good points.
- Thoughtful and insightful.
- The value of this session is to understand that what is happening in the United States and Canada is also happening in Europe and reinforces the ideas we are hearing at the conference. I have come to know Spanish, French, and even English books

---

[121] The original assessment in English is available at http://www.argelich.com/wp-content/uploads/2013/05/Conference-evaluation-Orlando-2011-Agustin-Argelich.pdf

I should read. It also helps to review aspects we already know or do.

- Agustín is a fascinating man and a great contribution to our organization. He offers a different view and forces us to take some time to look at our work from a different angle. What a refreshing session!
- Wonderful message and perspective.
- Good use of videos and graphics.
- Interesting, good references.
- Inspiring.
- Very interesting, it is always good to remember the basics.
- Different, creative, fun.

Conferences

Overview of international conferences, where the author has lectured on the contents of this book:

- London, UK; March 2014. Connected Business Expo "Deploying and Managing Multi-National Unified Communications."
- London, UK; February 2014. Oil & Gas Mobility Summit (2nd edition). "How to design the best mobility solutions and how to lead and manage with success mobility projects in the Oil & Gas industry."
- London, UK; March 2013. Unified Communications Expo "Moving forward: building a culture of continuous improvement."
- London, UK; February 2013. Oil & Gas Mobility Summit:
  o Cutting-edge strategies to lead successfully mobility projects.
  o Improving business-processed efficiency through mobility and Unified Communications and Collaboration's (UC2) customized deployments.
  o Baltimore, USA; October 2012. STC Fall Conference: "Unified Communications and Collaboration international deployment. Lessons learned."
- Amman, Jordan; November 2011. Princess Sumaya University for Technology JISER-MED. Conference on Quality Assurance, Employability,

and Internationalization: "The Power of Collaboration."

- Orlando, USA; October 2011. STC Fall Conference "Moving Forward. Building a culture of continuous improvement."
- Seville, Spain; June 2011. IT Trade Mission. The US in Andalusia. "Cutting-Edge Strategies to Build an International Network of Partners and Friends How can a small company do it? Why must a small company do it?"
- Tokyo, Japan; November 2010. 21st Congress of the International Federation of Hospital Engineering: "Unified Communications and Collaboration – an essential tool for hospital operations."
- San Jose, California, United States; August 2010. E-mobility summit.
  o Cutting-Edge Strategies for Internally Training your Mobile Workforce With Newly-Implemented Technologies.
  o Avoiding Organizational Chaos and Cost With Growing Workforce Mobility Need.
- Barcelona, Spain; October 2008. 20th Congress of the International Federation of Hospital Engineering: "Developing network strategies to support hospital operations. Telecom Networks, a hospital's nervous system."
- Mexico City, April 2008. World Union of Wholesale Markets. "Developing network strategies to support market operations" conference.
- San Francisco, USA; October 2006. STC Fall Conference "Bringing 21st-Century IT Solutions to an 18th-Century Business."

Index

Abel   76
Ah Puch   159
Alberich, Lluís   263
Alonso Puig, Mario   72, 243
AMP   260
As-built drawings   188
Ascó, NPP   60
Augustine, Saint   89, 90
Bankinter   98
Barcelona '92, OG   87, 205
Benedict of Nursia   83
Benedict XVI   75, 107
Borges, Jorge Luis   76
Boyd, John R.   147, 241
Breslow, Michael   226
Burka, Jane B.   79
Business model   229
Buyer, Martha   13
Cain   76
Caution   187
Chambers, John   98
Chaplin, Charlie   182
Chernobyl   204
Cisco   98, 260, 261, 262
Cleary, Thomas   145, 272
Competitive intelligence   147
Covey, Stephen   206, 228, 235
Coworking   228
CTCA   49
Cuba   107

David, king 160
Delgado, Perico 249
Disciplined collaboration 217, 227
Edholm, Phil 79, 98, 229
Eiger 200
Ek Chuah 158
Fernández Ochoa, Paquito 210
Flowchart 226
Francis, Pope 27, 107
Frankl, Viktor 207
Fukushima 60
Giuliani, Rudolf 208
Gladwell, Malcolm 129
Gödel, Kurt 148
Goliath 160
Gray, John 93
Gregory the Great, Pope 75
Hansen, Morten T. 217
Heisenberg, Werner Karl 148
Hertfelder, Eduardo 28
Hitler 182
Holy Spirit 83
Husserl, Edmund 58
Hutchison, William 245
Incompleteness theorems 148
Indurain, Miguel 249
Influencing 80
Itxab 159
Jankowski, Mark A. 160
Jesus of Nazareth 102
John Paul II 108, 114
John XXIII 162
Kennedy, John F. 106, 125, 162

Khrushchev, Nikita   162
Lazarus   82
Learning organization   72
LinkedIn   233
Lose-lose   157
Maier, Corinne   28
Maister, David   253
Malthus   26, 253
Marina, José Antonio   75, 76
Martha and Mary   82
Martínez Porcell, Joan   87, 90
Mercabarna   257
Missile crisis   162
Mobile World Congress   49, 98
Mussolini   182
Napoleon   76
Niebuhr, Reinhold   91
Olivé, Lluis   204
Omission   73, 80
On-going management   200
OODA loop   241
Orange   260
Parable   102
Parker, Marty   225
Pay per use   80
Pérez-Díaz, Víctor   28
Pérez, Josep Lluís   149
Peter Pan   88
Philosophy   108
Pontius Pilate   85, 96
Power   80
Procrastinating   79
Purnell, John   94

Ramírez, Miguel   239
Ribeiro, Lair   95
Rodríguez, Juan Carlos   29
Sartre, Jean Paul   58
Self-destruction   159
Senge, Peter   272
Shapiro, Ronald   160
Siemens   260
Solomon   77
Sony   260
Stein, Edith   58
Sun Tzu   147
Tapscott, Don   51
Technical specification   190
Technology watch   147
Teresa of Calcutta   82, 139
Thomas Aquinas   75
Three Mile Island, CN   204
Trías de Bes, Fernando   211, 272
Tulum   158
Uncertainty principle   148
Unified communications   48, 225
Vegetating state   105
Venice   209
Vitek, Christopher J.   229, 273
Vodafone   261
Welfare state   105
Welfare State   27
Win-lose   157
Win-win   157
Wisdom   72, 77, 91, 107, 187, 217
Workflow   226
Yuen, Leonora M.   79

List of figures

Figure 1. Population pyramid of Spain
as of January 1, 2013.   34

Figure 2. Project management model
that ensures their quality control.   134

Figure 3. Malpractice scheme in project
implementation. The result quality
is not guaranteed.   135

Figure 4. OODA loop by John Boyd.   240

Figure 5. Continuous improvement
by repeating the Shewhart/Deming
cycle.   242

Figure 6. Intelligent Community Open
Architecture Tasting Model.   246

References

Alonso Puig, Mario. *El cociente agallas* (The guts quotient). Espasa, 2013.

Alonso Puig, Mario. *Vivir es una necesidad urgente* (Living is an urgent need). Punto de Lectura, 2013.

Burka, Jane and Yuen, Leonora. *Procrastination Why you do it, what to do about it Now.* Da Capo Press Books, 2008.

Covey, Stephen. *The 7 Habits of Highly Effective People.* DC Books, 2005

Covey, Stephen. *First Things First.* Free Press, 1996

Dans, Enrique. *Todo va a cambiar* (Everything will change). Deusto. 2010.

Edholm, Phil. *Napkin Logic 48 Great Business Ideas, Lessons, and Rules, and Insights to make you a better business person and entrepreneur.* PKE Consulting LLC./Createspace, 2014.

Frankl, Viktor. *Man's Search for Meaning.* Beacon Press, 2006.

Fernández Ochoa, Paco. *La vida, un slalom* (Life, a slalom). La Esfera de los Libros, 2008.

Ginebra, Gabriel. *Gestión de Incompetentes* (Incompetent people management). Libros de Cabecera, 2010.

Ginebra, Gabriel. *El japonés que estrelló el tren para ganar tiempo* (The Japanese who crashed the train to gain time). Conecta, 2012.

Guderian, Heinz J. *Panzer Leader.* Da Capo Press, 2001.

Hansen, Morten T. *Collaboration.* Harvard Business School Press, 2009.

Jabad, Alberto and Lorca Gómez, Julio. "Innovación no es lo mismo que novedad" (Innovation is not the same as new). *Andalucía Investiga*, 38: 44. 2007.

Johnson, Spencer. *Who Moved My Cheese?: an Amazing Way to Deal with Change in Your Work and in Your Life.* G. P. Putnam's Sons, 1998.

Lao Tse. *Tao Te Ching,* Harper Perennial, 1900.

Maister, David H. *The Trusted Advisor.* Free Press, New York, 2000.

Peppers, Don and Rogers, Martha. *The One to One Future.* Currency Doubleday, 1996.

Peppers, Don and Rogers, Martha. *Rules to Break & Laws to Follow.* Wiley. Microsoft Executive Leadership Series, 2008.

Pérez-Díaz, Víctor. *Alerta y desconfianza. La sociedad española ante la crisis*. (Alert and distrust. The Spanish society before the crisis). Confederated Savings Banks Foundation (FUNCAS), 2011.

Khadem, Riaz. *Total Alignment*. Infotrac, 2008.

Kranz, Eugene. *Failure Is Not an Option: Mission Control From Mercury to Apollo XIII and Beyond*. Simon & Schuster, 2009.

Senge, Peter. *The Fifth Discipline: The Art & Practice of the Learning Organization*. Currency Doubleday, 1990.

Shapiro, Ronald M. *Bullies, Tyrants, and Impossible People: How to Beat Them Without Joining Them*. Crown Business, 2007.

Sun Tzu. *The Art of War*, version by Thomas Cleary, Edaf, 2006.

Rojas, Ignacio. *Qué se sabe de... Los símbolos del Apocalipsis* (What do we know about ... The symbols of Revelation). Verbo Divino, 2013.

Trías de Bes, Fernando. *El hombre que cambió su casa por un tulipán (The man who changed his home for a tulip)*. Temas de Hoy. 2009.

Tapscott, Don. *Wikinomics*. Portfolio Trade, 2010

Tapscott, Don. *Grown Up Digital*. McGraw-Hill, 2008.

Vitek, Christopher J. and Edholm, Phillip E. *WebRTC for Enterprises: History and Use Cases*. Create-Space, 2014.

Reference books

Amela, Víctor. *Antología de citas. Sabiduría humana en 30.000 sentencias* (Anthology of quotations. Human wisdom in 30,000 sentences). Styria, 2010.

Clyton, Mike. *Management models pocketbook*. Management Pocketbooks Ltd., 2008.

Dyer, Wayne W. *Your Erroneous Zones*. William Morrow Paperbacks. 2001.

Dyer, Wayne W. *Wisdom of the Ages*. William Morrow Paperbacks, 2002.

Fernández Aguado, Javier. *1000 consejos para un emprendedor* (1000 tips for an entrepreneur). CIE Dossat 2000, 2000.

Fernández Aguado, Javier. *Proverbios para la empresa* (Proverbs for the company). CIE Dossat 2000, 2000.

Hunter, James. *The Servant: A Simple Story About the True Essence of Leadership*. Prima, 1998.

Marina, José Antonio. *Por qué soy cristiano* (Why am I a Christian). Anagrama, 2005.

Marina, José Antonio. *Pequeño tratado de los grandes vicios* (Small treatise of the great vices). Anagrama, 2011.

Nouwen, Henri J. M. *Return of the Prodigal Son. A Story of Homecoming*. Image Books/Doubleday Publishing Group, 1994.

Peters, Thomas. *In Search of Excellence: Lessons from America's Best-Run Companies*. HarperBusiness, 2006.

Ratzinger, Joseph. *Introduction to Christianity*. Ignatius Press, 2004.

Roig, Xavier. *Ni som ni serem* (We neither are nor will be). La Campana, 2002.

Roig, Xavier. *La dictadura de la incompetència* (The dictatorship of incompetence). La Campana, 2008.

Seewald, Peter. *Salt of the Earth: The Church at the End of the Millennium – An Interview With Peter Seewald*. Ignatius Press, 1997.

Seewald, Peter. *God and the World: A Conversation With Peter Seewald*. Ignatius Press, 2003.

Recommended authors

Apart from the reviewed books, all works of the following authors are interesting.

- Alonso Puig, Mario
- Covey, Stephen
- Dyer, Wayne E.
- Frankl, Viktor
- Fernández Aguado, Javier
- Gray, John
- Marina, José Antonio

Acknowledgments

To my wife, my children, my parents, my siblings, my parents-in-law, my siblings-in-law, and my many nephews and nieces, especially my three goddaughters, Inés, María, and Lali, for their backing, support, and enthusiasm in this project.

To my grandparents, Agustín and Carmina, Javier and Josefina, for having overcome much more difficult times than the ones we have gone through.

To my team at Argelich Networks.

To my friends and colleagues of the Society of Communications Technology Consultants International.

I appreciate the voluntary and involuntary, known and unknown collaboration of all people who, with their example and advice, have helped me write this book. Some do not know how influential they have been: Ignasi Martínez Porcell, Jaume Solé, Enrique Mur, Josep Pallarès, Juan José Josué, Josep Maria Ligorio, Jordi Maymó, Augusto Alegret, Lluís Alberich, and David Albalate.

I also think it is fair to mention my main spiritual advisors at different stages of my life: Father Ignasi Armengou and Father Antoni Deulofeu, priests of the Catholic Church of the Dioceses of Barcelona and Egara (Terrassa).

I would like to express my particular gratitude to those who put their trust in my collaboration when I started off my career, with a special remembrance of some who are no longer down here with us, such as Jaume Ollé.

www.ingramcontent.com/pod-product-compliance
Lightning Source LLC
Chambersburg PA
CBHW051856170526
45168CB00001B/124